HOW TO WORK WITH COMPLICATED PEOPLE

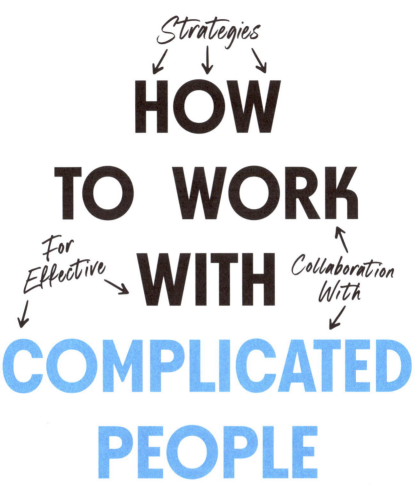

How to Work with Complicated People

Copyright © 2025 by Ryan Leak

All rights reserved. No part of this publication may be reproduced, stored in a retrieval system, or transmitted in any form by any means, electronic, mechanical, photocopy, recording, or otherwise, without the prior permission of the publisher, except as provided by USA copyright law.

No patent liability is assumed with respect to the use of the information contained herein. Although every precaution has been taken in the preparation of this book, the publisher and author assume no responsibility for errors or omissions. Neither is any liability assumed for damages resulting from the use of the information contained herein.

The stories and examples that appear in this book come from the author's interviews, consulting, and research. The names of individuals, companies, and other identifying facts have been changed to protect the identities of those who provided them, and any resemblance to actual individuals is merely coincidental. Some interview and research responses have been edited for brevity and clarity.

Published by Maxwell Leadership Publishing, Nashville, Tennessee.
Distributed by Simon & Schuster.

Library of Congress Control Number: 2024913933

Print ISBN: 9798887100432

E-book ISBN: 9798887100449

Cover and interior design by Rodrigo Corral Studio

Printed in the United States of America

To John C. Maxwell,

This book would not be possible without your generosity, insight, and leadership. Your intentional life and legacy have inspired me to consistently seek ways to add value to the world around me. Thank you for showing me how to take the high road and for teaching me to see beyond what people are to who they can become. Because of your dedication to your craft and legacy, you've paved the way for someone like me to stand a little taller and dream a little bigger.

With deepest respect and admiration,
Ryan Leak

CONTENTS

1. THE PERSON YOU NEED THIS BOOK FOR — 2
2. GOOD, BETTER, AND NOT-SO-BAD NEWS — 32
3. STOP LETTING THEM SURPRISE YOU — 52
4. SAME PLANET, DIFFERENT WORLDS — 72
5. COLLABORATION IS A MINDSET — 90
6. PEOPLE QS — 114

7	AGE IS JUST A NUMBER... UNTIL YOU HAVE TO WORK TOGETHER	146
8	NOW YOU'RE SPEAKING MY LANGUAGE	166
9	THE CUSTOMER IS NOT ALWAYS RIGHT	204
10	DON'T SHOOT THE MESSENGER	222
11	PUTTING THE "NEARLY" IN NEARLY ANYONE	242
12	CHOICES THAT CHANGE YOU, EVEN IF PEOPLE STAY THE SAME	266
	CONCLUSION	286
	ACKNOWLEDGMENTS	289
	ENDNOTES	291

CHAPTER I

THE PERSON YOU NEED THIS BOOK FOR

The minute you saw the title of this book, there's a good chance the name of a specific coworker, boss, or employee ran through your head.

Why? Because in every workplace, while you're trying to navigate change, pursue audacious goals, and manage your work-life balance, there lurks a more daunting challenge: dealing with complicated people.

You know the types. The overbearing boss who can't decide if they're a micromanager or an absentee leader. The colleague whose mood swings could give the stock market a run for its money. The client whose demands rival those of a diva on a world tour.

Welcome to the wild, wild world of working with complicated people—a journey as unpredictable as it is unavoidable.

You don't need a book to tell you that complicated people are making your job hard. What you need, and what I'm here to share with you, is a survival guide not just for enduring these individuals but for thriving among them. This isn't about changing them, because—spoiler alert—you can't. Rather, it's about changing how you interact with them. My goal is to give you strategies to help you effectively work with nearly anyone. (We'll get to that "nearly" part later.) It's to help guide you through the minefield of complicated characters and prickly personalities in the workplace.

As an executive coach and speaker, I've had the opportunity to speak and consult all over the world. I work with numerous Fortune 100 clients, professional athletic teams, and leaders in just about every sector you can imagine—from the glitz of sports and entertainment, to the number-crunching world of finance, to the meticulous realms of insurance, pharma, and manufacturing. I even spoke at an eyelashes professionals conference not long ago. (Yes, there's an entire micro-industry just for lashes within the larger beauty world, and they're crushing it.)

Wherever I go, I take notes, and it's clear that complicated people are found in every workplace. Regardless of the industry, location, or size of their company, my clients and audiences consistently complain about the handful of challenging individuals who drain their energy, test their patience, and make them question their career choices.

I've concluded that one of the greatest hurdles to loving your job isn't what's in the job description itself, but who you work with. The difference between wanting to stay at your company forever and secretly shopping your resume on indeed.com often boils down to a specific person or group you work with or for. These individuals either make your job feel like a life calling . . . or a life sentence.

After all, you spend a lot of time at work—about half of all your waking hours during the week, assuming eight hours of sleep and an eight-hour workday. Throughout your lifetime, you can expect to spend between 85,000 and 90,000 hours at work.[1] No other activity except sleep even comes close to that. Obviously, the more you can do to make those hours enjoyable, productive, and fulfilling, the better.

One of the biggest variables in that equation is the quality of your human interactions. Complicated people can make or break your work experience.

DEEP DIVE INTO COMPLICATED

So, what does it mean to be a complicated person? After all, the term *complicated* isn't exactly a technical measurement.

My real-world definition is this: it's the individual who popped into your head when you read this book's title. It's the name or face your mind jumps to the second you hear the word *complicated*.

That particular person is complicated to *you,* and that's what matters most. So go ahead, think about it for a second. Who is the most complicated person you work with? I doubt the answer will take long. You'll immediately have a picture in your mind of that individual. You'll know their name, gender, approximate age, eye color, and possibly body odor.

We all have complicated people in our lives, and the challenge isn't just how to describe them but how to deal with them. That's the challenge that occupies our minds and spikes our blood pressure, and it's the journey we're going to take together in the following pages.

To better understand the scope and impact of complicated people in the workforce, my team and I conducted a comprehensive national research study of 1,000 working Americans, including full-time employees, part-time employees, and self-employed individuals ages 18–65.[2] Some were old-school and worked with complicated people in person, some worked with complicated people virtually, and some did a bit of both. The study was weighted to the 2020 U.S. Census for age, region, gender, and ethnicity, and it has a margin of error of +/- 3.1 percentage points, which means it gives an accurate snapshot of the American workforce today. We asked people detailed questions about everything from how many complicated people they work with to how these interactions affect their performance, mental health, and job satisfaction.

My team and I wanted to develop effective, research-driven strategies that can help you work with almost anybody. And the data blew us away. It confirms what I see in my day-to-day experience and hear in my conversations: complicated people are holding you back. They're holding us back. We'll unpack more of our findings later on, but some of the highlights include:

COMPLICATED PEOPLE are a widespread problem. Nearly 1 in 2 Americans (46%) say they deal with complicated people daily or multiple times a day in the workplace. A whopping 78% say they deal with them at least weekly. More than 3 of 4 working Americans (77%) agree that complicated individuals are a serious problem in most work cultures, while 85% say it is important to the success of their job to be able to work effectively with these individuals.

COMPLICATED PEOPLE are affecting our work in every way imaginable. Our survey showed dramatic effects on workplace efficiency and experience, with complicated people being responsible for worse communication, lower morale, eroded unity and trust, lower job satisfaction, and much more. Nearly 1 in 2 workers say regularly dealing with complicated people would make them hate their job. Workers regularly change their habits to avoid complicated people or situations, including skipping days of work, and many (44%) have quit jobs due to complicated bosses.

COMPLICATED PEOPLE are harming our mental and emotional health. Within the last year, two-thirds of working Americans (67%) report experiencing high levels of stress as a direct result of working with complicated individuals. Other negative effects include anger, bitterness, frustration, hopelessness, loss of sleep, depression, fear, anxiety, and personality changes. A terrifyingly high number of people report having clinically diagnosed mental health issues (18%) and suicidal thoughts (11%) within the last year due to working with complicated people.

These aren't just statistics; these are people. People like you and me. People who go to work every day and often struggle to navigate the complexities of interpersonal relationships.

Here's the biggest concern. When we asked people how often they experience a positive resolution to the challenges of working with complicated individuals, 30% said they rarely or never experience it, and another 38% said they only do sometimes. Only 31% of people "often" or "constantly" experience a positive outcome to their complicated-people challenges.

Considering how many complicated people are out there and how often we're interacting with them, that's not great. It's dismal, actually. It means the majority of us are going about our jobs every day, dealing with a lot of complicated people without a lot of success.

Along with the survey, I also conducted phone and virtual interviews with a number of my clients and contacts who are C-suite leaders and key stakeholders, including several Fortune 100 companies and a couple of professional sports franchises. I picked their brains on the best strategies for moving *toward* people we'd rather avoid. (I've changed their names and titles so you can't guess who they are. You can try, though.) And of course, I've spent countless hours poring over books, research papers, and other material produced by experts in the various fields of study represented in the chapters ahead.

All of that to say, this book isn't just theory. It's the evidence-based, experience-driven result of quantitative data and qualitative input from observations and conversations across many industries. I'm confident it will help you engage more effectively with the people you're blessed, cursed, or doomed to work with, whatever the case may be.

This brings me back to the question I asked above. What makes the people you work with complicated? Why do certain people spring to mind so quickly?

"How would you define or describe a complicated person, coworker, or leader at work?" was one of the core questions we asked people in our study, and their answers ranged from hilarious to heartbreaking. For example:

- **"Someone who is hardheaded and can't admit when they are wrong."**
- **"A pain in the rear end."**
- **"Someone who forgets or doesn't know what it's like to be the little person."**
- **"Someone who steals our stuff a lot and then gets mad when we confront him about it. Like bro, quit stealing!" (That one definitely has a backstory.)**

Many respondents described the characteristics of people who felt complicated to them. They tended to be specific, practical, and easy to imagine, and I found myself nodding along as I read through them.

- **"Doesn't show up for work or slacks off at work."**
- **"Doesn't want to listen to anyone else even if they are wrong."**
- **"Not open-minded and a terrible listener."**
- **"Lazy; on their phone constantly."**
- **"SOMEONE THAT NO MATTER WHAT THEY ARE ALWAYS MISERABLE AND NEGATIVE."**
  (Yes, this one was in all caps.)

There were some common themes in our research study. Words like *stubborn, hard, difficult, annoying, attitude, communication*, and *bossy* popped up all the time.

When we asked people to choose the top three characteristics they most associated with complicated people, the main ones they identified were, in this order: *Unwillingness to change, learn, or grow; overly negative, critical behavior; laziness or a poor work ethic; poor communication skills*; and *manipulative behavior.* All five of these were highlighted by at least a third of the respondents.

So yes, complicated people share a lot of similarities…but they are also wildly unique. The reality is that part of what makes this tricky is the infinite, infernal combination of "complicatedness" that exists out there in the wild.

And you have to figure out how to work with them.

SO WHAT'S THE GOAL?

When it comes to defining our goal in the pages ahead, let me start by saying what this book is not. First, it's not about gaslighting yourself into staying in a toxic environment or making you take the blame for everyone else's problems.

You probably have a rock-solid list of reasons why certain coworkers deserve the *complicated* label. Maybe they harmed you, stole your ideas, sabotaged your project, or lied about you to your boss. Only you can know who is safe and who is not, so I'm not going to tell you to blindly believe the best about someone who has a bad habit of twisting a knife into your back.

Second, it's not a book about "fixing" that person, or controlling them, or magically turning a complicated individual into a simple one.

The only person you can change is yourself. Reading a book and expecting it to change someone else is like taking medicine and thinking another person will get better.

Rather, we're going to focus on making your workplace collaboration as effective as possible. I want to give you strategies and mindsets that can help you see better results with less pain. You should be able to work with (nearly) anyone and not lose your sanity or humanity in the process.

I want to show you that just because someone is complicated to work with doesn't mean they're bad, wrong, or hopeless. It doesn't make them "difficult to work with" in the negative, dismissive sense. *Difficult* can come with complicated, but it doesn't always.

Often, they're just complicated. And that's okay. Complicated is not an insurmountable obstacle.

Actually, it can be a gift. The beautiful thing is that the process of learning to collaborate with complicated individuals is transformative. You'll get to know yourself better, and you'll grow in your understanding of the wildly diverse world around you. That can't help but change you for the better. As you'll see, it's often an essential gateway to greater creativity, stronger teams, and increased productivity.

On the other side of complicated is the wonderful, wide-open world of effective collaboration and a workplace you love.

That's the goal we're aiming for: successful, productive teamwork and collaboration. It lies at the heart of everything we're going to explore ahead.

To achieve that goal, you might need to do something different than what you've done to date, especially if you're in the two-thirds of people who aren't seeing a lot of success in this area.

You need solid strategies in order to collaborate effectively with different kinds of individuals—the picky, pokey, prickly ones in particular. The spicy ones and slimy ones. The nasty ones. The people who get on your nerves and under your skin. The individuals whose mere names trigger sighs and eye rolls when they pop up in your inbox. The ones you've given "special" nicknames to in your phone contact list.

We're going to get to those strategies in the pages and chapters ahead. But first, I need to make an important point, one that is a hidden key to unlocking the enigma of people around you. If you don't understand this, no amount of tips, tricks, or tools is going to help you. It's not just "those people" who are difficult, unique, complex, and confusing. It's not just that boss, that client, that coworker, who is complicated.

You are complicated too.

YOU ARE COMPLICATED TOO.

SOMEBODY'S IDIOT

Fun fact: I recently petted a dog for the first time in my life. I'm not exaggerating. It was literally the first time I have ever voluntarily shown affection to a dog. I can't help it—I'm terrified of them. If you have a dog, I will not visit your house. Period.

In this case, I made an exception because the person I was visiting had an incurable disease, so it seemed petty for me to refuse to visit for something as superficial as a pet phobia.

I quickly found out they didn't just *have* a dog; they *loved* their dog. They couldn't stop talking about their dog. So when the hairy little beast walked up to me and wanted attention, I could not, in good conscience, do what I really wanted to do, which was recoil in disgust and push him away forcefully with my foot. As an act of love and supreme sacrifice, I petted him.

I'm just not a pet guy. Sorry if that offends you. But that's me.

Here's another random fact: I enjoy keeping my car and my house clean. And by *enjoy,* I mean *obsess over.* I wash my car every single day. I find deep inner tranquility in a freshly vacuumed floor.

Because of this, I'm also a cleaning products gadget guy, something my wife thinks is hilarious. I will compulsively purchase and bring home random mops, brushes, and other cleaning tools. Our vacuum cleaner looks like it was designed by NASA. It has an LCD touchscreen, it vacuums *and* mops the floors, and it's capable of landing a rover on the moon.

I have no problem cleaning the house right in front of visitors. We'll have twenty friends over at our house hanging out, and at 8:30 p.m. I'll pull out my emotional support vacuum cleaner and fire it up mid-conversation. I'm not sending people a message that they should go home. I'm sending them a message that they should help clean.

I'm a clean freak. I'm sorry if that bothers you. That's me.

I could keep going about my funky, quirky, and irritating idiosyncrasies—and you probably could too. Not about mine, I mean, but about your own. We all have them. We all laugh at them or loathe them. But for better or worse, they are part of our current mental, emotional, and social makeup.

When it comes to dealing with challenging individuals in the workplace, we have to start by looking at ourselves. Welcome to complicated, my friend. You are part of the problem.

We don't naturally think this way. Every time I tell somebody the title of this book, they say something along the lines of, "Oh, yeah, I need that book. You should see some of the clowns I work with."

I reply, "And I bet somebody else needs the book for you!" Then they laugh and nod their heads because they know it's true.

One of our findings that made me laugh out loud was this: 74% of people think they are less complicated to work with than the average person. That's not how averages work, though. Clearly, while we're often very aware of how complicated *other* people are, we are decidedly less aware of how complicated *we* might be.

Here's another one that made me laugh, but in a morbid way. We found that at least 1 out of every 2 workers (57%) has a coworker, manager, or client at work who "constantly needs to be saved from the drama and complications they create." This means there's a high probability you're working with someone like that.

And if not…well then, statistically speaking, *you* are that person.

I'm kidding. Mostly.

When it comes to working with complicated people, it's easy to hyperfixate on other people's quirks and complications, to believe that our workplaces and jobs would be better if everybody else just changed. It's easy to feel like we're surrounded by complicated idiots who need to get their acts together.

But the only way we'll ever work well with them is by accepting a hard truth:

We are all somebody's idiot.

We are all weird, odd, irritating, or baffling to someone else.

Let that sink in for a moment. I know *they* are complicated, but you won't understand them until you first realize you are one of them. While you're sipping your coffee and mentally drafting that "how to be less complicated" manual for your colleagues, someone else is doing the same for you.

The other day I saw a social media post by author and speaker Mel Robbins: "The truth is, none of us are easy to be with."[3] It's simple, brutal, and true. We confuse some people. We frustrate some people. We irritate some people.

That doesn't excuse ignorance or wrong behavior on our part, but it does put things in perspective, doesn't it?

You're complicated.

I'm complicated.

We're all complicated.

You're

C😮MPLICATED

↑ I'm   ↑ We're all

There is humility in recognizing this, and there is also freedom in it. Freedom to work on ourselves and to give space to other people to do the same. Freedom to meet in the middle or to find a third option when there are clashes, rather than insisting that another person becomes someone they are not so our lives can be easier.

Really, this comes down to having enough humility, honesty, and self-awareness to admit that any discussion about how complicated *they* are must start with how complicated *we* are.

Author Alain de Botton writes, "We have a bewildering array of problems that emerge when we try to get close to others. We seem normal only to those who don't know us very well. In a wiser, more self-aware society than our own, a standard question on any early dinner date would be: 'And how are you crazy?'"[4]

In context, he was writing about dating and marriage, but the same goes for networking events. *Hey, Terrance, here's my crazy; tell me about yours.* The closer you work with someone, the more you both become aware of each other's quirks. Maybe job applications should include a line that says, "And how are you complicated?"

If I were to introduce myself honestly to people,
it would go something like this:

HI, MY NAME IS _Ryan_
AND I'M COMPLICATED.

I'm complicated to work with because I consistently have multiple irons in the fire.

I'm hard to read.

There are moments when I'm crystal clear on what I want from my team, but sometimes I honestly don't know what I want or need until I see it.

Sometimes I'm extremely present in the room, but sometimes I'm thinking about that other iron in that other fire that urgently needs my attention.

I'm an introverted person with an extroverted career.

I'm moodier than I'd like to admit.

I love humans, but I'm allergic to happy hour and small talk.

I'M JUST...COMPLICATED.

That's only a brief glimpse of me. I could go on for multiple paragraphs, and I'm still understanding how complicated I am. I'm also still learning to accept it and give myself grace for it. But I realized a long time ago that if I can't start by recognizing my own idiosyncrasies, it's going to be extremely difficult for me to be effective in working with others.

We have to silence the inner narrative that says *they* are the problem, *they* need to change, *they* are hard to work with, and *they* are being unreasonable. What if we switched up the subject of those sentences?

Maybe *I* am the problem. Maybe *I* need to change. Maybe *I* am hard to work with. Maybe *I* am unreasonable.

Those phrases might be wrong…but they might be at least partly right. You won't know until you ask yourself if they are true, though. And you won't ask yourself until you remember that you are complicated too.

That's scary. That's humbling. But that's healthy.

One of the most important keys to working with difficult individuals is having a keen awareness of our complications *while also* making space for the complications of others. It's not either/or. It's both/and.

We have to constantly remind ourselves of that because it's all too easy to look at other people as if their complications were the problem and our "simplicity" were the solution. We treat them as problems to be solved rather than as humans to be understood. When we do that, though, we miss the magic in the mess—the magic in *their* mess, in *our* mess, and in the beauty we could create if we learned to mess things up together.

This is not easy, which is why so few people get good at it. If you and that other guy are both complicated human beings, it stands to reason that your working relationship is going to be challenging at times. But the answer isn't to pretend you are perfect and they are the problem. It isn't to steamroll their personality, mock their strange habits, judge their defects, or wish *they* would change so *your* day could be smoother.

It's to learn strategies for dealing with complicated people. And that starts by remembering—with humor and humility and self-compassion—that we are all somebody's idiot.

YOU'VE GOT OPTIONS

Once you've accepted the reality of your own complexity, you're a lot more prepared to engage with other complicated people.

For many of us, that's a daily—if not an hourly—activity.

Think about all the people who cycle through your workday: clients, customers, coworkers, bosses, employees, executives, independent contractors, partners, shareholders, members of the media, consultants, auditors, board members, donors, inspectors—the list is almost infinite.

If you work with people in any capacity—which includes pretty much anyone with a job—some of those people are not going to be easy to figure out. They have issues. They have quirks. They have dark sides and downsides.

You can't change this fact.

So, what are you going to do about it?

While there are countless strategies you might employ to deal with complicated people, these strategies can be divided into four general categories:

OPTION I:
Avoid Them

What is the easiest way to deal with a difficult situation? Pretend it doesn't exist and hope it goes away. When faced with someone who baffles you, you might think: *If I avoid them, maybe they'll leave me alone. If I ignore them, I won't have to deal with them. Problem solved.*

A lot of people choose this option. In our survey, we found that 61% of working Americans are constantly or often avoiding complicated individuals at work. In sports and entertainment, that number rises to 84%, the highest of any industry we tested. In communications and media, it's 78%. That is a lot of time, energy, and emotion spent dodging difficult people.

I get it. Ignoring or avoiding someone might provide short-term relief. Plus, by choosing not to engage, you might even believe you're keeping the peace or preserving your energy.

The problem is that life doesn't really work that way. Avoiding or ignoring issues doesn't actually solve them. Most of us are stuck with these complicated coworkers, bosses, or employees anyway, so we can't ignore them even if we want to. They're in the next office over, or they are our direct report, or they just got promoted to office manager.

Avoiding problematic people might be a temporary fix, but it isn't a viable long-term solution.

OPTION 2:
Change Them

This is often our go-to strategy. When we have creative brainstorming meetings with ourselves to plan how we're going to deal with a complicated person, our brightest idea is usually to get them to change and think more like us. Then, in subtle ways, we pull, push, and prod them toward our preferences. There is a word to describe that, and it's a word no one wants to describe the way they work: *manipulation*.

Trying to change someone is an option, but I don't necessarily think it's a smart one.

You've probably been on the other end of being pulled, pushed, and prodded in a direction you didn't want to go, and I'd be willing to bet it didn't feel good. The arm-twisting strategy rarely works because nobody likes having their arm twisted. Besides, even if you do force someone to change, nobody actually wins. They'll resent you for operating with an iron fist, and you'll know they modified their behavior only to avoid a conflict with you.

Plus, it's really not possible to change people from the outside. It's hard enough to change yourself, and you're on board with your own ideas. It's pretty much impossible to talk someone else into changing something they don't want to change. You can't control their opinion of you, their personality, their value system, their worldview, their phobias, their communication style, their bad breath, or their bad habits. Those things and many more are outside your lane and above your pay grade.

Genuine change is a personal journey, and no one likes to be coerced or manipulated or gaslit into it. So, while changing them is technically an option, I don't think that movie ends with them wanting to work with you.

OPTION 3:
Cancel Them

I was working with a leader one day, and I asked him about a previous employee I considered to be a mutual friend of ours. He said, "Them? Oh, they're dead to me."

His response surprised me. *Dead?* Really? What did they do to merit the cerebral and emotional funeral you gave them?

In an age of digital interactions and fleeting relationships, "canceling" someone has become as casual and common as declining a Facebook event invitation. It essentially means writing off anyone who doesn't agree with you or whose opinion doesn't align with your worldview. This could mean cutting ties, no longer being on speaking terms, ending the relationship altogether, or, even worse, advocating for their exclusion from groups or the company. It can easily move from *you* canceling them to you believing *everyone else* should join you. It's a slippery slope from "I don't like you" to "Nobody should like you."

Just as most people don't enjoy having their arm twisted, most people don't want to be canceled. Plus, I find there is usually a bit of a double standard in our rules for the cancellation of others versus how we treat ourselves and want others to treat us. As author Stephen M. R. Covey wrote, "We judge ourselves by our intentions and others by their behavior."[5] It might be human nature to give ourselves the benefit of the doubt while we hold everyone else to a higher standard, but that doesn't mean it's healthy.

The tendency to cancel difficult people leaves us with interesting math:

THEY HURT ME = THEY DESERVE TO BE CANCELED.

But when we hurt someone else and they're upset, we want different math:

I HURT THEM = I DESERVE A PASS BECAUSE....

I was sick.

I was stressed.

I had a bad hair day.

My company restructured.

I lost a family member.

I was going through a divorce.

I had so much pressure on me.

We subconsciously assume that we have a valid and legitimate story, but they have no excuse to bring their "complicated" to the office. We want other people to give us the benefit of the doubt for very nuanced, valid issues they are unaware of, but we'll write them off completely for their confusing behavior without stopping to ask if maybe, just maybe, they deserve the benefit of the doubt too.

While there are certain situations in which setting boundaries or cutting ties is necessary for your well-being (see Chapter 8), using cancellation as a primary strategy is limiting, to say the least. Using disconnection as a default isolates you from a work community you could be collaborating with to make your job a better place to work. When you shut out people who have different ideas and beliefs, you halt your development, sabotage healthy dialogue, and perpetuate division.

Again, it's an option—but it's not a healthy one.

OPTION 4:
Understand Them

This isn't the easy option. It is the *growing* option, though, and it lies at the heart of this book. Embrace the chaos, my friend. Consider the most complicated person you work with and look for a way to approach them, understand them, and connect with them.

I know it may be hard, but you don't buy books about how to do easy things. The ability to learn to do hard things is what separates elite people from normal people and great leaders from average ones.

You are hungry to learn how to *work with* that person who is so confusing, frustrating, abrasive, or difficult to work with.

NOT HOW TO:

→ work against them

→ work around them

→ get them fired

→ prove them wrong

→ pretend they don't exist

Those things might be okay for regular people, but I'd argue they are not okay for growing people. They are not okay for people who want to push beyond the immediate reactions of irritation and frustration so they can reap the rewards of genuine teamwork.

Understanding people better is a learned skill, and that's good news. Why? Because it means you can get better at it. You can grow in it. While it's difficult to move toward someone you'd rather move away from, if you want to excel and be effective in your life and career, becoming competent at connecting with different kinds of people is one of the key skills that will help make that happen.

Choosing the option to understand complicated people allows you to initiate open dialogue, ask questions without judgment, and actively listen. It enables you to see the world through their eyes, and that makes your world bigger. You won't agree with them on every point, but you can still acknowledge their humanity and their right to have their own perspective while simultaneously recognizing that your knowledge of them (and of the rest of the world) is partial at best. Again, that's humility.

Understanding is what we all seek, isn't it? It's what we hope someone would do for us before ignoring us, trying to change us, or canceling us altogether. This is of utmost importance because I guarantee that you work with at least one person who feels misunderstood. You've been there too. We all have.

While writing this book, I presented some of the research to a team my company works with. During the Q&A portion of our time together on Zoom, a woman named Lucy confessed that she often felt like the "complicated" one in her office. Intrigued, I wanted to dig deeper. Lucy explained to all of us on the call that she's deaf in one ear. People at work would walk by on her deaf side, say hello, and she wouldn't respond because, well, she couldn't hear them. Naturally, they assumed she was just being rude.

Afterwards, I spoke with one of the leaders. He was shocked by what he'd learned. "I've known Lucy for eight years," he said, "and I never knew." Think about that for a second. Eight years of misconceptions, awkward moments, and probably a fair share of office gossip, all because Lucy felt she couldn't share her story.

I get it. Vulnerability is tough. But when Lucy finally opened up, her team got a chance to truly understand her. Just like that, the "complicated" label started to peel away. Lucy wasn't complicated; she was misunderstood. All it took was a bit of bravery on her part to start changing that narrative.

This experience reminded me that everyone has a story. And sometimes, the people we label as complicated are just waiting for the right moment to share theirs. When we create environments where people feel safe enough to be vulnerable and honest, we unlock a whole new level of connection and understanding.

Think about a time you've been misunderstood. Can you remember what it felt like to be in that position? Maybe your boss didn't appreciate your ideas on a project, your coworkers didn't like how you did your job, or an employee who worked for you got mad about a decision you made. At that moment, what did you wish they would have taken the time to do? Listen to you. Understand you. Give you the benefit of the doubt. Untangle your "complicated" and see the world through your eyes.

You probably didn't expect them to completely agree with you (although that would have been nice), but you at least wanted them to engage with you from a place of authenticity rather than dismiss you with a label or a laugh. Let's extend that grace to others. In a complicated world, the best thing we can do is try to understand each other.

One of the more encouraging findings from our study was that when we asked people which of these four strategies (ignore them, change them, cancel them, or understand them) they used most often, the highest response was consistently "understand them." Of course, as I mentioned earlier, the success rate for resolving the problems that complicated people cause is quite low overall.

What does that mean? At least in part, I think it indicates we know we need to understand complicated people, but we don't necessarily achieve that understanding.

That's the point of this book. We want to get better at the individual strategies, tools, mindsets, and actions that build bridges of understanding.

The word *with* in the title, *How to Work with Complicated People,* is really the linchpin of this whole thing. It's an easy word to skip over, though. It's not even capitalized in titles because it's a lowly preposition. But *with* is a powerful term. It's a connecting word. A teamwork word. A relationship word. It means you're on the same side and share a common goal. That might be hard to believe when your complicated colleague is messing with your mind and your plans, but my invitation here is simply to get better at this. To improve. To grow wiser and move closer.

Don't just tolerate a toxic status quo until it drives you to a meltdown, a beatdown, or a breakdown. Instead, do what you can to understand who they are, where they are coming from, what they are trying to accomplish, what makes them tick, and how you can build a bridge to their world. Even if that person never changes, you can change, and that could make all the difference.

You probably figured it out already, but this chapter title was a setup. "The Person You Need This Book For" . . . is you. Not just because you are somebody's idiot (no offense), but because you can't change anyone else, and no one else can change you.

The power is in your hands. The choice is up to you. No one can force you to truly, sincerely, effectively work with complicated people. You have to decide not to take the "easy" road of ignoring them, canceling them, or changing them and instead learn to understand them.

When you do, you move one step closer to collaboration. Of course, when you're dealing with a challenging individual who seems to have made it the mission of their life to complicate yours, there might be moments when you wonder, *Why even bother trying to work with this person? I don't want to collaborate with them. I want to drop-kick them into another time zone.*

That's a good question. Is effective collaboration with complicated people really worth the hard work and vulnerability it requires? After all, it's not like you get a pay bonus for every person you learn to wrangle or untangle. (Wouldn't that be nice, though?) Short answer: yes, it's worth it. You actually have a lot more influence than you might realize, and with a little effort and understanding, you can reap a long list of benefits. That's what we're going to explore next.

"THE PERSON YOU NEED THIS BOOK FOR" IS <u>YOU.</u>

CHAPTER 2

GOOD, BETTER, AND NOT-SO-BAD NEWS

My first job was at a shoe store called Finish Line in a Rockford, Illinois, shopping mall when I was eighteen years old. That's where my sneaker addiction began too. My paycheck essentially went straight back to the company because I'd spend all my money on shoes.

One day a woman came into the store, and I sold her a pair of running shoes. To my surprise, she offered me a job at a clothing store she managed in the same mall. I ended up working part-time at both stores. It was chaotic but also hilarious because sometimes I would sell shoes to a customer at one store and then sell them a dress shirt an hour later at the other store. My favorite response to their confusion was to pretend I was a twin.

A few months later, one of my managers at Finish Line got a new job at a Best Buy down the street, and he asked me if I'd go work for them because they needed extra holiday help. Suddenly, I had three jobs at the same time within a one-mile radius. There was a three-month period when I could sell you Jordans, jeans, and a juicer all in the same day.

Not only was that season my introduction to the workforce, but it was also my introduction to how complicated work can be—especially working with people. The three companies had completely different products, cultures, values, hiring processes, and leadership styles. But the biggest challenge of all was learning to deal with the constant, ever-shifting rush of customers I dealt with every day.

Later, I left the part-time chaos behind and embraced full-time chaos as an employee at a headhunting firm, helping organizations fill executive roles. That was a whole new level of complicated. Working in the human resources department is like trying to juggle flaming swords while riding a unicycle on a tightrope. You're the middleman between employees and management, dealing with everything from hiring to firing, benefits to conflicts. You have to be a therapist, detective, and diplomat all rolled into one.

I've worked at a few other places since then, and I've also started businesses of my own.

I've spent the last few years as an executive coach and a keynote speaker for Fortune 100 companies, which has given me a front-row seat to learning about leadership challenges across a wide variety of industries. In the two decades since I was sprinting between three part-time jobs, a couple of things have not changed: first, my love for sneakers; and second, the reality and the complexity of working with people.

Robots have not yet taken over the world, which means no matter which company any of us work for or what kind of business we run, we are going to be working with people. Some of those people will be complicated. To be fair, *all* of them will be complicated in one way or another.

You can't opt out of working with complicated people because to be human is to be complicated. You might wish you could work in a perfect world, where you hire only perfect people, sell only to perfect people, and work only for perfect people, but you can't. First of all, you wouldn't be in that perfect world yourself. And second, nobody else would be there either.

We are complex, nuanced beings with detailed backstories, occasional bad days, and tenacious big dreams, and we bring our complicated selves to work every day. No one just shows up at eight in the morning, works till five in the afternoon, then ceases to exist until the next morning. We all have a home life, a work life, a leisure life, and a love life—or at least we'd like to have them.

That means we might be sitting in a meeting, but we're also reserving some energy for our evening plans or the weekend ahead. We're probably dedicating some mental resources to the fight we had with our spouse last night or the new roof we need to put on our house. And if you and I are doing those things, doesn't it stand to reason the other people sitting around the boardroom, break room, or green room are doing the exact same thing?

Ultimately, most of the difficult things you deal with during an average day probably come down to people. I know that org charts and spreadsheets and budget meetings and product launches and balance sheets are also convoluted and complex. But there are real people behind all of those things.

Nearly all work-related problems are people problems, at least to some extent. They either involve people, depend on people, or affect people. This means if you want to get better at working with difficult people, you need to get better at people in general.

You don't have to magically morph into a social butterfly if you're a lifelong introvert, but regardless of your personality, getting better at working with people is crucial to your success and theirs. Get a PhD in what it means to be human. Read, study, ask, learn, empathize, grow, and connect until you can look past the complications and see real, living humans who are just trying to keep their life together while working on their marriage, parenting toddlers who think they are teenagers (or teenagers who behave like toddlers), or dealing with the occasional bout of existential dread.

Here's the thing: human beings aren't problems to be solved. They certainly have problems, and they definitely *cause* problems, but they are people. And at the end of the day, people matter most.

If you can remember that these challenging individuals are first and foremost human beings

—NOT PROBLEMS, ISSUES, OR COMPLICATIONS—

you'll find it easier to work with them.

WHY BOTHER?

Considering how complicated we all are, you might be wondering if it's even worth it to strive for better teamwork and collaboration. Sure, complicated people deserve respect and understanding, but can't you just do that from a distance? Preferably waving goodbye to them as they exit your office space permanently?

No, you can't.

As we saw already, complicated people are everywhere. They are as inevitable as dings in your car door or red lights when you're late to work.

But don't grudgingly resign yourself to working with certain people just because you can't escape them. For one thing, that's a depressing way to look at it; but more importantly, it ignores the *benefits* that come from learning how to work with them effectively.

Benefits? What benefits could you possibly gain from doing the hard and often thankless work of building bridges rather than burning them?

A significant portion of our research focused on answering that question. We didn't want to conduct a national survey just to prove that complicated people are everywhere and they're driving us all crazy. I mean, that might be the case, but it's not very inspiring.

Instead, we wanted to know how people's work experience would change if they were able to become more effective at understanding and interacting with complicated people. The results were clear: workers believe every aspect of work we tested, from job satisfaction to productivity to innovation, would improve.

To be honest, we expected to find that. It aligns with both common sense and the real-world experience we all bring to the table.

But here's something we didn't expect to find, something that gives me hope and confidence that we can get better at this and therefore gain those benefits: the number of people who are spoiling your work experience is probably less than your emotions might lead you to believe. They just have an outsized impact.

> **The vast majority of people (84%) regularly work with 1 to 5 complicated people. That's a relatively small number of individuals.**

They make a lot of noise.
They create a lot of drama.
They occupy a lot of your therapy sessions...
BUT THERE ARE ONLY A LIMITED NUMBER OF THEM.

Think about how much hope lies in that fact, my friend. If you get better at dealing with this small, specific group of people, you'll likely see a dramatic improvement in your work experience.

This is doable. It takes work and growth, but the benefits are real.

So, what are the benefits? Why should you get better at collaborating with complicated people? In answer to that question, I have some good news, some better news, and some not-as-bad-as-it sounds news.

LET'S START WITH THE GOOD NEWS.

GOOD NEWS:
YOU'LL LOVE YOUR JOB MORE

> **According to our study, almost half of American workers (47%) report that complicated individuals "very negatively" or "negatively" impact their job satisfaction, while another 41% say they "slightly" or "somewhat" negatively impact it. That means for nearly 9 out of 10 people, getting better at collaborating with challenging colleagues will likely lead to higher job satisfaction...*even if nothing else changes.***

That puts the power back in your hands.

Earlier, I mentioned you might spend between 85,000 and 90,000 hours at work in your lifetime. It would be terrible to hate those hours, wouldn't it? However, many people do exactly that. They view work as a necessary evil, something to be endured so they can get the paycheck they need to live, so they can go to work, so they can get paid, so they can live, so they can work, so they can get paid . . .

Is that really what you want, though? If you're going to be working anyway, you might as well do what you can to improve the experience. That includes figuring out how to work with the complicated people who are draining your time, joy, and energy. You might love what you do, but if you hate who you do it with, it's going to blow up your job satisfaction.

You didn't need research to tell you that, of course. You've probably been telling it to your coworkers, spouse, or friends. "If Miguel would only get transferred, we could get twice as much done with half as much drama." "If Sarah would only get herself fired, my life would be so much easier."

> **In our recent study, 75% of people agreed complicated individuals are "creating a crisis of stress and frustration in the workplace."**

When we quizzed people about the specific pain points complicated people created, they unloaded on us. At the top of the list were communication problems, morale issues, loss of unity and trust, and poor job satisfaction, closely followed by negative impacts on mental health, productivity, engagement, focus, employee retention, and innovation.

When we asked about behaviors people were likely to engage in when dealing with complicated individuals, avoidance topped the list, followed by losing trust in management, hating their job, and losing trust in their company. There was also a significant group of people who identified avoiding specific meetings, quitting or considering quitting their jobs, adjusting their work hours, requesting a transfer, or not giving their best effort.

The emotional and mental impact of complicated people, which I referred to earlier, was one of the most alarming results. We found over half of respondents had dealt with high stress levels, anger or bitterness, and frustration or hopelessness in the last year due to complicated people. Over a third struggled with loss of sleep, depression, fear or anxiety, or even personality changes. Many more had experienced bullying or emotional abuse, sought therapy or counseling, been clinically diagnosed with health issues, or experienced suicidal thoughts.

Other studies on interpersonal conflicts at work have found the same thing: when people have higher rates of conflict, they tend to enjoy work less. These interactions can be one of the primary reasons people want to quit their jobs.[6] Clearly, complicated people are causing real problems for everyone.

Here's the thing: Miguel and Sarah might not be going anywhere anytime soon. But if you improve your connection with them (or whoever is haunting your headspace or office space), your job satisfaction will almost inevitably rise because *they were the ones helping tank it in the first place*. That's what I mean by getting your power back.

BETTER NEWS:
YOU CAN IMPROVE YOUR WORKPLACE

If you can pull this off, you'll make your company a better place, both for you and for those around you. This isn't just about enjoying your job more but about helping other people enjoy theirs too.

People often think their companies would be a better place if the benefits were better, if they had more stock options or bigger bonuses, or if there were more opportunities for professional development. Those things would be nice, but they may or may not be within your power to change. Our research indicates, however, that reducing the problems associated with complicated people could improve every facet of work we tested: communication, morale, unity and trust, mental health, productivity, engagement, and more.

Again, that gives you the power back. How? By allowing you to improve your workplace, one positive interaction at a time. Don't underestimate the power of these interactions to change the people around you, whether you have the title of "leader" or not.

I often tell groups I speak to that company morale is determined one interaction at a time. When you're a new employee, the first email you receive begins to shape the story you tell yourself about the company. If the first email is rude, then "people here" seem rude. If the first meeting allows space for quiet voices and personalities to be heard, then "people here" are inclusive.

Whether you realize it or not, somewhere out there, people are telling themselves a story about your workplace based on your behavior. Is it a good story or a bad one? A healthy one or a toxic one? A collaborative one or a complicated one?

You and I have the power to change people's perceptions of the workplace we share, one interaction at a time. We can't change the entire company overnight, but we can work on the interactions we do have some control over, particularly the ones with complicated people.

When we asked people what makes individuals complicated to work with, "attitude" was the winner by a mile, with 68% listing it as one of the top three characteristics they associate with complicated people. Here's the thing: attitudes are contagious. You've probably caught a bad one from somebody a few times, and maybe you've caught some good ones.

There's a social network theory called Three Degrees of Influence, which states that our influence on other people extends to three circles—or degrees—of connection. It was proposed by social scientists Nicholas Christakis and James Fowler, who write:

"**EVERYTHING** we do or say tends to ripple through our network, having an impact on:

one degree — **OUR FRIENDS**

two degrees — **OUR FRIENDS' FRIENDS**

three degrees — **AND EVEN OUR FRIENDS' FRIENDS' FRIENDS**

Our influence gradually dissipates and ceases to have a noticeable effect on people beyond the social frontier that lies at three degrees of separation. Likewise, we are influenced by friends within three degrees but generally not by those beyond."[7]

This means that whether you're the life of the party or the office introvert, you have massive influence. Let's say you have twenty interactions each day, and all those people have twenty interactions with different people, and each of those people has twenty more human connections. Based on this theory, in one twenty-four-hour period, you could have some degree of influence on *eight thousand* interactions.

Remember, nearly everyone in our survey reported dealing with 1 to 5 complicated individuals regularly in the workplace. Just think of how many people those few individuals represent. If you learn to use those moments of interaction to nudge the needle in a better direction, you could potentially benefit not only those specific complicated colleagues but also their circle of contacts and their circle's circle. Ultimately, you could help defuse dozens of negative interactions because you knew how to interact in a healthy, positive, uplifting way with a handful of cranky folk.

I once spoke to 2,500 pharmacists at an event sponsored by the American Pharmacists Association. Now, I don't know what your experience typically is at pharmacies, but for most people, I think it's similar to the DMV or the post office: nobody wants to be there, and everybody is in a bad mood. They're only there because someone is sick, and they're just hoping the doctor entered the prescription correctly and their insurance covers it.

I was talking to these pharmacists about leadership and about changing the morale and environment where they worked, and I could almost read their thoughts: *What do you want us to do? People are sick. It's depressing. Of course everyone is in a bad mood.*

I told them the first question I typically get asked at a pharmacy is: "Date of birth?" No greeting, no smile, just "Date of birth?" while the pharmacist pokes away at their computer screen. The second question is usually: "Insurance?" And on it goes until I get my medicine and make my escape.

I said to the audience, "What if you looked the customer in the eye and asked sincerely, 'How are you feeling?'"

By the looks on their faces, you'd have thought I had just announced we were going to launch a spaceship to Mars at the end of the session. I told them that just because people were grumpy and other pharmacists were stressed didn't mean they couldn't create change by taking simple steps to connect with people.

Often when I'm speaking, I'll illustrate how easy it is to make a difference by asking people how many of them have ever had their half-birthday celebrated. In a room of a thousand people, maybe thirty will raise their hands. So I'll say, "That's 3%. So next time it's someone's birthday, go forward six months in your calendar and make a note. When their half-birthday rolls around, send them a text or give them a cupcake. There's a 97% chance they'll say, 'I've never worked at an organization that celebrated my half-birthday before.' That's how easy it is to make a difference. It's a matter of choosing to use your influence for good."

NOT-SO-BAD NEWS:
YOU NEED THESE PEOPLE

Finally, this might sound like bad news, at least at first, but it really isn't: *you need complicated people.* Maybe not all of them, but many of them. You depend on them, learn from them, and work better because of them.

That might seem like bad news because you probably wish they'd retire or quit. But in the long run, many of these complicated connections will work in your favor if you learn to collaborate more effectively.

I don't just mean you need them to get their job done so you don't have to do it. I mean they can actually add value to your work and to your world. You need them in your life. They might have some bad traits, but they have something to contribute too.

I've noticed it's often hard for us to admit we can learn or receive anything from complicated people. That's why I called this "bad" news. It feels bad because it challenges our inner need to make them villains. We'd prefer to cancel them and move on. Admitting that we need them feels contradictory, confusing, and maybe even humiliating.

This isn't a dismissal of your pain, because you've probably correctly identified the ways this person or these people are screwing up your workday or messing with your mind and emotions. Instead, it's an invitation to recognize they might not be all bad. Very few people are. And very few people, if any, are all good. We are each a bit of both.

The fact that you see them as complicated usually means they are different than you in some way, and that means they probably offer something you don't already have. If you can figure out how to work *with* them rather than against them, your unique strengths and perspectives will often complement each other and create a better result than either of you would get on your own.

Differences are not always easy to deal with, which is why the first instinct of many people can be to stiff-arm or strong-arm anyone who is too different. If we push them aside or hold them down, they won't get in our way.

But is that really what you want?

For people to just stay out of your way?

Sure, that does sound kind of nice—at least at first. But hopefully, you can see how small of a world that would create.

We're all wildly different, and that is inherently beautiful. Everyone brings their suitcase packed with emotions, backgrounds, and personal stories into those Monday meetings. You are collaborating with people whose childhood stories are wildly different from yours or who interpret a simple nod in a totally unexpected way.

This rich tapestry of experiences and perspectives is what makes us all unique, but it's also the reason Quinn from Accounting gets miffed when someone borrows his stapler, or why Riley in HR has a peculiar penchant for collecting rubber ducks, or why Harper from Shipping insists on sending her emails only in Comic Sans.

At the core of human behavior, there are different invisible drivers: things like ambition, ego, and the ever-present resistance to change. That means some people you deal with are fueled by their dreams, others by their strong sense of self-worth, and yet others by a desire to find comfort in the familiar. Some people will love change, and some will eye any shift in routine with a touch of skepticism. Some will dream with you regardless of the obstacles, and others will want a detailed cost analysis and a step-by-step plan before they'll even consider that new product you're so excited about.

Add in the occasional external stressor, like an unexpected health crisis or the neighbor's cat who has taken up nocturnal opera singing, and you've got a potpourri of human experiences sitting around the same table.

And that's where the magic happens.

THAT'S WHERE
THE MAGIC HAPPENS.

In this crazy salad of human personalities, when everyone brings their intricate, mysterious selves to the table, you discover the secret sauce to killer creativity. Innovation is birthed at the crossroads where our distinct stories and quirks converge. Yes, there will be bumps in the road, but it's in embracing these unique differences that we breathe life and energy into our collective efforts.

The rich diversity and beautiful unpredictability of humanity turn the challenge of working with complicated people into a courageous journey of discovery. In other words, *it's good to work with people like this.* It's not always easy, but if you do it right, you can learn to not only tolerate or understand the complications, but to value them, learn from them, and collaborate with them.

Once you see the value in complicated people, I think you'll start seeking out individuals you don't understand because you're curious to know what *they* see that you don't. Instead of viewing complicated people as competitors and giving them the old Heisman stiff-arm, you'll lower your guard and treat them as collaborators. You'll ask questions that go beyond simple workplace issues because you care about what makes them tick. You'll find yourself overlooking a few inconveniences and awkward comments because you value their perspective and unique way of thinking.

We'll explore the benefits of differences, diversity, and disagreements in the chapters ahead, so for now, just remember this: *complicated people can be really, really good for you.* They can be the answer to problems you couldn't solve and obstacles you would never be able to overcome on your own.

If your knee-jerk reaction to someone's wonky attitude or actions is to shake your head and wonder, *Why do I always get stuck with the weirdos?* you're going to miss out on the gifts buried beneath that wonkiness. To receive the benefits they offer, you have to embrace the complications they bring.

I know that sounds about as appealing as embracing a cactus. But wise, growing, exceptional people can see past the prickliness and value the contribution of the person underneath.

So again, why should you get better at working with complicated people? Why not just ignore them, cancel them, or force them to change?

- **First, because you'll enjoy your job more.**
- **Second, because you'll make your workplace better.**
- **And third, because you need them.**

People are complicated, but they are worth understanding. That's a lesson worth remembering and a goal worth pursuing.

CHAPTER 3

STOP LETTING THEM SURPRISE YOU

Let's talk about Baron, a fast-paced, high-powered pharma executive in Chicago who found most people lazy. Well, he didn't actually believe they were lazy; he just saw them as lazy compared to him. He knew he had high expectations, but his version of leadership was demanding the impossible before nine in the morning and being baffled when everyone else just wanted to finish their coffee.

You've seen the type—the one who thinks a cape and a superhero landing are part of every job description. Baron put a lot of pressure on himself, and therefore he put a lot of pressure on his team. He often found himself expecting miracles from people who occasionally struggled to operate the espresso machine. He wanted a groundbreaking drug discovery by Monday, FDA approval by Wednesday, and viral marketing campaigns by Friday.

But instead of employees who performed superheroic feats, he was consistently met with regular human beings who had imperfections, emotions, and the audacity to need sleep. The gap between Baron's expectations and reality was as vast as the Grand Canyon.

One week, I was invited to speak at what Baron would later describe as "that fateful team-building retreat," designed to create camaraderie through sharing circles and group exercises. The group did a trust fall exercise, with Baron falling backward into the arms of his team members. He knew they'd catch him, and he assumed he'd feel their hands on his back as soon as he started tipping over. But he didn't. Instead, the team waited until the very last second before grabbing him and lowering him to the ground. The look of shock and panic on his face was priceless, and the whole team erupted in laughter.

That moment of levity, as quick and seemingly "normal" as it would appear to anyone else, had a profound impact on Baron. His team had always viewed him as stoic, serious, and all business. They'd never seen him rattled—or even a tiny bit *unpolished*—until that day, which meant they'd also never seen him be . . . *human*.

They'd created a lot as a team. They'd built a lot. They'd sold a lot. But they'd never laughed a lot.

Baron realized that simply allowing himself to be a little less perfect and a bit more human changed the entire team dynamic.

Returning to the office, Baron began experimenting with a different approach. He started expecting surprises, messiness, and the beautiful chaos of human imperfection. He didn't sigh or roll his eyes when a project meeting turned into a brainstorming session about alien invasions as a metaphor for market disruption. He joined in, contributing ideas about intergalactic regulatory compliance.

Baron started rolling with the punches. He stopped letting the disparity between his pace and theirs throw him off his game. Deadlines became more realistic. Meetings were less about mind reading and more about mind-blowing ideas, like using memes in presentations. The shift was subtle but profound. Colleagues started looking forward to interactions with Baron and began sharing ideas they would have previously kept to themselves for fear of falling short of his impossible standards. Creativity flourished, as did laughter and a sense of camaraderie that had been missing.

As Baron's executive coach, witnessing his transformation was like watching a supervillain discover they're actually a pretty decent karaoke singer. And so, in a world where perfection was the expectation, Baron learned to find joy in the imperfection, hilarity in the errors, and, surprisingly, effectiveness in embracing the chaos.

He changed his expectations, and that changed everything.

When we view people as "complicated," it's often because they don't meet our expectations. Something about them—their personality, their communication style, their manners, their leadership, their social skills, their behavior—doesn't match our inner definition of what is "right" or "normal" or "good."

THEY

mess with our rhythm, our goals, or our preferences

hurt our feelings

do things differently

slow us down

sabotage our work

frustrate us

disrupt our plans

get in our way

SO WE CALL THEM

COMPLICATED.

It's not that we're self-absorbed tyrants who think the world revolves around us, but we have work to do, deadlines to meet, products to design, paychecks to collect, careers to nurture, companies to build, and dreams to fulfill. The last thing we need is challenging individuals messing with our minds or our plans. My advice is this:

Don't let them surprise you.

This is up to you.

It's within your control.

Why do you keep getting surprised when people are complicated?

What could you do to be less shocked by their errors and humanity?

How could you, like Baron, learn to actually embrace imperfection and draw effectiveness from chaos?

I have a couple of suggestions. First, establish healthy expectations in advance. Expectations are key to how you experience anything.

Second, learn how your brain works when it feels threatened so you can hack your survival instinct and build bridges instead of walls.

We'll come back to the survival instinct conversation in a moment, but let's begin with expectations. If you don't want to be surprised by people, stop expecting the impossible from them. Let go of expectations that set them up for failure and set you up for frustration. In other words, go on an expectations detox.

GO ON AN EXPECTATIONS DETOX

Detox means getting something out of your system. Maybe you've tried a sugar detox by eliminating sweets or a social media detox by deleting X from your phone. It's a reset. A chance for your body and emotions to stabilize in a healthier place.

I'd like to propose putting yourself on an *expectations detox* when it comes to the most complicated people in your life by intentionally and honestly evaluating what you think they should do and why your expectations are so far off from the reality of how they show up. This is about reflecting on the role your values, habits, and needs might play in why they keep disappointing you. Maybe your expectations are totally reasonable and right . . . or maybe not. Or maybe "right" means one thing for you and another thing for them, and until you can wrap your mind around their way of seeing things, you'll keep getting surprised and shocked by them.

One time when I was talking with a client, they kept saying, "Well, hopefully my boss will change."

I replied, a little bit incredulously, "Why would that happen? What evidence do you have that makes you believe they are going to change when they don't think they need to?"

The person just stared at me at first, then smiled. It was a sad smile. He and I both knew the boss in question wasn't even trying to change. Rather than wasting time and energy on wishful thinking, this person needed to put the onus back on himself in this less-than-ideal situation.

We have to stop expecting people to change when they aren't even trying to change. If someone is on a trajectory of self-improvement, there will be signs. They'll send signals. They'll pay for coaching, a gym membership, a conference, therapy, or professional development. They'll read books or listen to podcasts. They'll ask questions. They'll actively leverage resources to grow.

A lot of people won't do that, though, because they think, *I'm good. Everyone else is the problem.* Don't mope around waiting for someone like that to change or meet your standards. You have higher standards for them than they do for themselves.

You know what *can* change? Your expectations.

Realistic expectations are key to any experience. Don't expect the impossible and then act shocked if you don't get it.

When it comes to dealing with people (all people, but especially certain ones), I cannot emphasize strongly enough the importance of setting the right expectations. That means assuming that some people will be reasonably or even unreasonably complicated.

I often do this when I'm about to have a phone call or meeting. I'll remind myself, *This probably won't be easy or smooth. They probably won't agree with me on everything. There might be some misunderstandings we'll have to work through. But it's okay if it's complicated. We'll just figure it out.*

It's a healthy habit because it keeps me from linking my definition of a "successful" call or meeting to happy feelings or good vibes. Something can be awkward and still be awesome. It can be messy and still be productive. As a matter of fact, it's usually all of those things at once.

Whenever you're interacting with another human, whether it's face-to-face, in a meeting, via email, or on a video call, stop expecting that it will be easy, that they'll see things your way, or that they will use only nice words and happy emojis. Don't let someone arrive at "complicated" in your mind just because you expected them to be simple and they turned out to be human, or because you were in a hurry for a quick resolution but they brought up an objection to your idea, or because you assumed their response time would be the same as yours but they had other priorities.

In particular, stop surrendering your emotional stability to people who fail to live up to expectations you failed to communicate. Putting unspoken expectations on coworkers is like holding them to a secret contract they never signed. If you make your expectations the final arbiter of what is good and what is bad, who is easy and who is complicated, you've given your imagination way too much power—especially if you've never even taken the time to put those fuzzy, subjective inner standards into words before.

Author Donald Miller writes, "When you stop expecting people to be perfect, you can like them for who they are."[8] Some of us need to take a little pressure off and just allow the people around us to be themselves. (And some of them need to do the same for us . . . but that's on them.)

Whenever you find yourself dealing with a complicated person, put yourself through a quick expectations detox, a reset, and make sure you're expecting the right things.

If they are thirty years older than you, is it reasonable to assume they'll grasp technology as quickly as you?

If this is their first job out of high school and they've never had a full-time job, is it logical to demand that they match your work ethic and knowledge level from day one?

If they're going through a divorce, is it even humanly possible for them to be emotionally balanced every moment of every day?

Having reasonable expectations is a protective measure for you. When you don't align your expectations with reality, you set yourself up for frustration and even offense. That's not fair to you or to them. Plus, if you hang your workplace satisfaction on whether other people make your life difficult or not, you're going to be very unhappy. You'll spend too much time and emotional energy focusing on how many times Boomer Bob or Millennial Madison got under your skin and on your nerves today.

So—and I say this kindly—get thicker skin. Get less-irritable nerves. Remember that most of them, most of the time, are just trying to survive too, so they probably aren't going to be too focused on your pet peeves or hurt feelings. That doesn't make them bad; it makes them human. Just like you.

I find that it's helpful to set my expectations in advance whenever possible. Think about driving, for example. I don't just hate rush-hour traffic; I loathe it. To be honest, I detest lines of any sort. Patience is not a virtue I was blessed with. I understand why some people put mannequins in the passenger seat and drive in the HOV lane. I'm not saying it's right; I'm just saying I understand it. So, when I know I'm going to be driving in traffic, I set my expectations low in order to be emotionally and mentally ready for the drama ahead. I'll tell myself, *Ryan, this is going to take a long time. Don't stress out. People are going to cut in front of you. People are going to forget what turn signals are. It's okay. It will all be over soon.*

It sort of works. I also have to put on a podcast or call a friend just to keep from focusing on the fact that I could walk barefoot on Legos faster than we're moving at the moment.

Do the same when you're working with people who seem a little complicated. Build room into your plans for their delays and mistakes. Don't remove the bar altogether, but don't set yourself and everyone else up for disappointment by placing it too high.

If you're presenting an idea or pitching a product, don't expect everyone to applaud or even agree with you. If you do, you're probably going to be surprised, and not in a good way. You might feel attacked, misunderstood, unsupported, or undermined. You might walk out grumbling about the complicated people around the table.

Adjust your expectations before the meeting. Remind yourself that you're speaking to fallible, emotional, busy, semidistracted, and possibly stressed-out human beings. Anything could happen, so prepare accordingly.

Do you see how this works? If you expect people to be complicated, you'll make room for it, and you'll think in advance about how you want to show up in that situation rather than being caught off guard and emotionally vulnerable. Whether it's a presentation, a board meeting, an email, a performance review, or just another day dealing with the office grouch, taper your expectations a little. Align them with reality.

INSTEAD OF

expecting simplicity	→	**get comfortable with ambiguity**
wishing everyone else would adjust their behavior	→	**adjust your expectations**
getting offended	→	**get curious**
resenting hassle and the "idiots" who cause it	→	**embrace the messiness inherent in all teamwork and creativity**
letting people surprise you	→	**try letting go of your preconceived ideas of what they will do, say, or think**

Remember as well that changing your expectations doesn't mean overlooking behavior that crosses a line. Actually, the opposite is true. One of the benefits of setting healthy expectations is that it allows you to identify when you are genuinely a victim of mistreatment and need to take stronger measures. If you are experiencing things such as harassment or abuse, you should absolutely seek help. The HR department, your supervisor or boss, and the legal system are there for a reason. Don't put up with abuse in the name of flexibility, grace, teamwork, unity, or any other "virtue."

When you find that your expectations have not been met, use it as a learning opportunity. Rather than getting mad at the people who let you down, consider what you might change in order to have better results going forward.

There's no shortcut to simple and no magic cure for complexity. Instead of wasting your time wishing you could find one, lean into the madness and messiness that come with being human. Detox your expectations and get comfortable with complicated.

TAMING THE WELL-INTENTIONED CATASTROPHIZER

The first key to not letting complicated people surprise you is to set realistic expectations in advance, as we saw above.

Here's a second key: recognize the triggers that set off your inner alarm bells.

In other words, notice when and why your brain sometimes categorizes people as difficult, challenging, weird, threatening, or otherwise complicated. Why? Because when it comes to evaluating people, it's easy to get things at least partly wrong, so you need to learn when and how to hack your brain's default reaction to danger.

Your brain's top priority is to keep you safe, but like an overprotective parent, it gets it wrong sometimes. It senses danger where this is none, or it tells you the sky is falling just because an acorn hit you on the head. In its zeal to keep you from harm, it often assumes anything different or unfamiliar is dangerous until proven otherwise.

That means you need to second-guess yourself sometimes. Don't just go with your initial emotional reaction when a complicated person's actions start to trouble you, terrify you, or tick you off. Your brain might be overreacting. Catastrophizing. Projecting worst-case scenarios.

Our brains love to tell stories that make us the heroes. In order for that to happen, though, we literally have to make stuff up. We can't truly see into someone else's mind or heart, so we conveniently fill in the blanks.

In her fascinating book *The Neuroscience of You,* Dr. Chantel Prat explains, "Using its different mechanisms for understanding the world, your brain builds a more concrete and complete *story* than it actually has the data to support. And I'm not talking only about how your brain interprets the stories it *reads*. I'm talking about the stories it *creates* as it produces your experience of reality."[9]

IN OTHER WORDS, whenever you deal with a complicated person, your brain is busy working in the background, piecing together data points (and making semieducated guesses about whatever it doesn't know for a fact) so that you can predict their behavior and stay safe. It's constantly evaluating things like:

→ **Is this coworker a threat?**

→ **Can this manager be trusted?**

→ **Is my boss in a bad mood today?**

→ **How do I get this client to buy my services or product?**

→ **How do I need to interact with my manager to get a raise?**

→ **How do I get that creepy guy to leave me alone?**

→ **What are the risks versus rewards of standing up to the office bully?**

These are difficult questions, and your brain never stops wrestling with them. It does this to serve you, to keep you safe and happy and comfortable, because that's what the brain is there for, and it's a full-time job. It's part of the reason your brain uses at least 20% of your body's resources despite being 2% of your body's weight.[10]

The problem is that *self-focused* activity isn't necessarily *self-aware* activity, which can lead to problems when you're dealing with complicated people whom your brain considers a threat. The infamous fight-flight-freeze response can be triggered by one weird email, one threatening comment, or one dark glare from someone across the office. Then, all too easily, your habits, hormones, traumas, and dramas start driving the bus, rather than your conscious mind.

Mature, growing people are aware of the things that trigger self-protection mode in their brain, and they know how to respond. Here are three triggers you need to watch out for:

I. DISCOMFORT

Some people are hard to work with, and "hard" can be interpreted as "wrong." Remember, your brain prefers to tell you stories that make you feel happy and heroic, but that's often a misguided survival mechanism. It might be dealing with the vulnerability and awkwardness you feel by saying, "It's not your fault. You don't have to keep putting yourself through this. Go find someone who thinks more like you. This person is just too hard to work with."

Are they, though? Or are they simply *harder* to work with, maybe because they're challenging your assumptions and confronting your blind spots? Maybe their dissimilarities and disparities are making your brain think, grow, and wrestle with some stuff . . . and it's whining a little bit about it.

Lean into the discomfort. Embrace the awkwardness. Allow the vulnerability and tension to exist without judging or hating it too quickly.

Sure, it can feel exhausting. When you don't understand someone or agree with their viewpoint or approach, you have to work harder to get things done, and everything can seem like a battle. It can also be embarrassing. It's cringe-inducing and emotionally risky to navigate differences. You feel like you're stepping on their toes or they're stepping on yours all the time. It's uncomfortable and vulnerable.

None of that is inherently wrong, though.

If you think about it, most new things, including good ones, are a little uncomfortable at first. Job interviews. Making friends. First dates. New hobbies. Getting a new pet. But those things are worth it, so you push past the discomfort, knowing you won't always feel that way. And over time, it gets better.

2. UNCERTAINTY

The human psyche is hardwired to be suspicious of new things. What is unknown might be a threat, and it's better to be safe than sorry. This is a subconscious, instinctive response. One researcher suggests fear of the unknown is a "fundamental fear" for humans.[11]

This instinct is good. It helps protect you.

For example, I'm cautious with food I can't identify. I'm not eating anything until I know what it is and where it came from, especially if it's one of my kids who is offering it to me. I've learned the hard way that "close your eyes and open your mouth" rarely ends well.

The problem is that people who are drastically, dramatically different from you can feel threatening to your subconscious self just because they are unknown. They might end up being the sweetest, smartest people you'll ever have the pleasure of working with, but when you first try to collaborate, your brain takes one look at their hairdo, communication style, or personality, yells, "Stranger danger!" and dials 911.

Tell your subconscious self to calm down a little. They're probably not dangerous. They might just be different. If you want to receive the gifts hidden in their differences, you'll need to override that reaction by engaging the rational, cognitive side of your brain.

The person who makes you nervous today might become your favorite coworker by the end of the year. They might keep you from making a really dumb mistake. You might learn something new by working with them. Your world might grow. They might tell really good jokes. They might have a gift for working well under pressure. They might be personal friends with Taylor Swift's manager's friend's dog's vet's accountant and can get you tickets to a sold-out show.

But you won't know how good or bad their differences are until you lower your guard enough to let them in, at least a little. Only then can the uncertainty be replaced with actual knowledge.

There's no hurry here. You can be cautious *and* curious. You can be wise *and* open. These things are not mutually exclusive. Don't show them where you hide your spare house key just yet, but don't assume they're a threat simply because they see the world or the project you're working on differently.

Unfamiliarity doesn't have to equate with suspicion. When your brain nudges you toward fear, push back with curiosity.

3. LACK OF CONTROL

As part of its relentless campaign to keep you safe, your brain likes to be in control. Even if you aren't a certified control freak, it's human nature to want to reduce risks by controlling the environment.

Complicated people are hard to control, though. You can't understand them, so you can't predict them. And if you can't predict them, you can't prepare for them or protect yourself from them. They are loose cannons rolling around the ship, and that puts everyone in danger of getting body parts blown off.

Those are real problems. Your brain is making some valid points. But again, it might be exaggerating a little.

Are they really as dangerous as your control-focused subconscious is suggesting? Maybe they aren't loose cannons. Maybe they're just aiming in different directions than you might have aimed. Right now, they're scary because they seem volatile, but if you put in the effort, you can probably start to figure them out.

Plus, is control the answer? For that matter, is control even possible? The answer to both of those questions is the same: probably not.

Just as with the human instinct to be suspicious, the instinct to control is one that sometimes needs to be overridden. Relax a little. Let the person be themselves. You don't have to label and judge them. You don't have to decide if they are too loud, too quiet, too strong, too nosy, or too defensive. Take that pressure off yourself.

Curiosity goes a long way here. When you're curious about someone, you no longer feel compelled to control them. You can look at whatever target their cannon is aiming at and be grateful they saw something you didn't.

No two people are alike, so fully understanding or controlling people is impossible. If you're waiting for that to happen before you relax and enjoy your team, you're going to be waiting a long time. Part of the beauty of the human race is our uniqueness, after all. Instead of being nervous when you can't predict or control the people you work with, learn to appreciate their complex humanity. Let them live it and express it with less judgment and more wonder.

These three things—discomfort, uncertainty, and lack of control—are fight-or-flight triggers that most of us deal with on a regular basis. When they kick in, pay attention to them. Don't hate them; they're keeping you safe. Just remember, though, that you might need to talk those feelings down out of a tree sometimes.

Don't let complicated people surprise you. Rethink and reset your expectations until they're aligned with reality, and override your fight-or-flight responses by engaging curiosity. Not only will you enjoy work more and deal with less drama and trauma, but you'll open yourself up to the gifts hidden in other people's differences.

Expecting people to be complicated is a great first step to dealing with these individuals who occupy so much of your attention. It puts you in a better headspace to interact with them. But is that it? Should you merely resign yourself to the reality of working with people who drive you crazy?

Short answer: no.

The step after *expecting* complicated is to *reframe* complicated. It's to rethink the story I mentioned above—the story you're telling yourself about them and your complicated relationship. That's what we're going to explore next.

CHAPTER 4

SAME PLANET, DIFFERENT WORLDS

Whenever I work with professional sports teams, I love to talk to GMs and coaches about their rosters. They'll often share with me which players have great potential, which ones are leaders in the locker room, and sometimes which ones are driving them crazy.

One time a member of the coaching staff for an NBA team mentioned a particular player we'll call Michael, who was especially difficult to deal with. I knew who he was talking about because Michael had a reputation in the sports world and the media.

A year later, as I was doing research for this book, I interviewed the same coach. I asked him if he had any complicated players, and the first person who popped into his head was Michael. That didn't surprise me. What surprised me, though, was what he said next.

"I'm all the way in love with him now."

"Really?"

"Yeah, I've gotten over my initial . . . whatever. He is complicated, but I feel like I understand him now."

I was shocked but also fascinated. "What changed?"

He replied, "I needed to approach our relationship with some humility and just try to figure him out. What is he thinking? What is making him tick? Why is he acting this way? I found out that it comes from the purest place possible. His default is always going to be to do more, to work harder, to go harder, to go faster."

The coach kept going for five more minutes, unpacking how he'd had to reevaluate his own perspective. Here is just a portion of what he said:

> **I PROBABLY LET SOME** of the narrative around Michael from previous people seep into my head, which isn't right. If you take a girl on a date, are you going to call her ex-boyfriend first? He'll say that she's going to drive you nuts, which is a terrible headspace to carry into your first date. But when you trade for players, that's what happens. You get all this intel from different places. But Michael isn't nineteen anymore, and I'm glad no one judges me on who I was when I was nineteen.

> That's part of my identity, but it's not who I am anymore. You grow, you evolve. It became very apparent to me that part of the problem was that I had preconceived thoughts about him, and I wasn't really trying to understand who he was in order to maximize him. Look, is Michael perfect? No, but he's on our team and I want to win, and I want him to win.

In one conversation, Michael was complicated. But in another conversation, my friend used words I'll never forget: "He's grown on me." I immediately wondered if I give the complicated people in my life the opportunity to do that—to grow on me. I'm sure you have some colleagues in your life who aren't fun to work with, but something powerful can happen when you allow them to grow on you.

What's interesting is that I left with more respect than ever for this particular coach, not to mention an entirely different perspective of the player. The coach had made a conscious choice to discover things that had been obscured by the baggage, narrative, and stigma that surrounded his player. He knew there was more to Michael's story, and he was willing to keep looking, to keep reading, to keep believing.

We all know there are two sides to every story, but we often don't make space for the second side. We look at people through the lens of our assumptions, the lens of their reputations, or the lens of our frustrations. Instead of recognizing the beauty that comes from interacting with someone else's world, we treat them like they're from another planet. Our differences become tools to polarize, ostracize, and dehumanize each other.

We may come from different worlds, but we share the same planet. We belong to the same species, the same human race. Rather than allowing our differences to divide us, we need to change the narrative in our heads. We need to tell ourselves a better, more generous, and more accurate story.

TELL YOURSELF A BETTER STORY

Being able to see the other side of someone's story is challenging because the stories we tell ourselves tend to be unplanned and unnoticed. Somewhere deep inside, we develop certain biases toward people, and those biases take intentional effort to unpack and discard.

In our national survey on working with complicated people, we noticed that people often have an emotional, visceral response to the complicated people in their lives. This was particularly obvious in their responses to one of my favorite questions: "How would you define a complicated person in the workplace?"

It was a straightforward, open-ended question, and we expected relatively neutral definitions, but a large number were anything but neutral. They were highly charged and very specific. You can hear in their responses just how frustrated and ticked off these responders were.

For example, one person wrote, "Female boss who thinks she's a god." I can almost picture the person who wrote that. Someone else said, "My leader is a guy named Nate, and he is funny and kind but lacks a work ethic." Another wrote, "This lady I work with named Leslie. She is hardheaded and old-fashioned." One respondent said, "I work at Target. It's full of complicated people." Another said, "I deal with the IRS on a daily basis. They are all complicated." Other responses included descriptions like "cantankerous," "Machiavellian," "numbskull," and, "really dumb."

Responses like these illustrate how often deep emotion is attached to the people we call complicated. Whether that emotion is justified or not isn't the point. The point is that preconceived ideas and deep-seated feelings cloud our judgment. They make it impossible for us to be objective. We need to have the maturity to name our emotions and inner biases and the humility to continually ask, "Is there another side to this story?"

Interestingly, even though the question was specifically asking for a definition, a number of people showed an impressive amount of self-awareness and empathy in their responses, which included:

- **"Someone who has stuff on their plate that I might not know."**

- **"My boss is rude on the job but kind away from work. She is a mother of three."**

- **"Someone who likely has experience with past trauma, likely from childhood."**

- **"Everyone carries an invisible backpack. We don't know what they carry on an everyday basis. Cut them some slack."**

- **"I would say they are an acquired taste or possibly a hard pill to swallow."**

I loved those comments. They reveal people who are not only struggling with complicated interactions but also willing to look past the emotions and discomfort and try to understand the person better. Rather than just labeling and discarding someone, they used empathy to try to understand the person a little better.

In my book *Leveling Up: 12 Questions to Elevate Your Personal and Professional Development*, I discuss the concept of biomythography, which refers to the stories we tell ourselves about ourselves. We typically cast ourselves as the hero of our own story, while other people are the supporting cast and/or the villains. Meanwhile, the people around us are doing the exact same thing . . . but they are the heroes in their own stories, while we are the supporting characters or villains.

Why do we do this? Because we all see ourselves as heroes. And if our situation or behavior contradicts that self-perception, we look for ways to relieve the pressure, to deal with the cognitive dissonance. Often, that means rewriting other people's stories or filling in the blanks with our own assumptions in ways that keep our personal hero status intact.

In books and movies, there is a technique called "unreliable narrator" in which the story is told through the eyes of someone who may or may not be telling the truth. They might be an alcoholic, have a mental illness, or actually be a villain, but since they are telling the story, the reader is left guessing what is truth and what is fiction.

When it comes to the stories we tell ourselves about our complicated coworkers, sometimes we are unreliable narrators. After all, we're the scriptwriter, narrator, and hero. It's only natural that we'd see the world through an us-tinted filter. But those stories can't give the whole picture because they are told from and seen through our own points of view.

One of my favorite books is *The Stories We Tell Ourselves* by Dr. Scott Gornto, a family therapist. He argues that the quality of our lives and relationships is directly and deeply influenced by the internal conversations we have with ourselves. While those conversations often contain elements of truth, they are usually skewed in our favor. Dr. Gornto writes,

> **MUCH OF THE PAIN** in relationships can be traced back to the stories we tell ourselves.... When we can begin to listen to our internal monologue and identify the irrationality of the stories we create, we can then become much more proactive about the way these stories affect, and infect, our relationships. In time, learning to differentiate between the fiction of our minds and the truth of our relationships will lead to less anxiety and more peace, less worry and more trust, fewer broken relationships and more healthy bonds.[12]

The good news is that we can often improve our connection with even the most complicated people simply by changing the narrative in our heads. This is not playing mind games but rather having perspective. How you see anything dramatically influences your relationship with that thing, and complicated coworkers are no exception. The great thing about this tool is that it is completely under your control. *They* don't have to change in order for *your* experience to improve.

In her book *Rising Strong*, bestselling author and researcher Dr. Brené Brown refers to the "hypothesis of generosity," which she describes this way: "What is the most generous assumption you can make about this person's intentions or what this person said?"[13] It's about giving people the benefit of the doubt. It means jumping to the best conclusion rather than the worst. Dr. Brown adds that while generosity should not be a free pass for people, when it's connected to a healthy understanding of integrity and boundaries, it can be both effective and liberating.

When it comes to collaborating with complicated people, try starting with a hypothesis of generosity. Maybe that short-tempered reply had nothing to do with you, and they're just tired. Maybe their crappy attitude is a result of a personal problem that's weighing them down. Maybe their irresponsibility is due, at least in part, to ignorance or inexperience, rather than a lack of character. Consider the reasons why their behavior is complicated, then see if you can imagine a story in which they aren't the supervillain.

Our default response, especially when we feel threatened in some way, is usually the opposite: we skip straight to a hypothesis of villainy. It's scary how quickly and subtly "they throw off my groove" can morph into "they are truly terrible people." The first is a statement of your experience, which is valid and valuable, but the second is a character judgment . . . and that's above your pay grade. Maybe they are terrible; maybe they aren't. You can't ignore the fact that your perception might be part of the problem. Your internal narrative might have hijacked your external relationship. In the interest of honesty and maturity, you have to keep that at the forefront of your mind.

They are difficult *to you.* They are complicated *to you.* Your opinion of them is subjective because there is no internationally recognized standard for difficult people, no objective scale for separating heroes from villains. At the end of the day, we're probably all a little bit of both.

Often, I find that the people who appear the most complicated to me are those who are the most different from me. We clash over our priorities, our preferences, our personalities, our perspectives. It's not that any of us are such terrible human beings, but we view things very differently, and those differences make us feel farther apart than we actually are. But what if we worked on expanding our groove a little, so we can connect and collaborate with a more diverse range of people? What if we told better, more generous stories about the "supporting cast" working alongside us—especially considering the fact that they are the main character in their internal story, and we are secondary characters to them?

When someone seems complicated to you, don't just slap a "way too complicated" sticker on them and move on. Instead, remember that you are perceiving them this way, but your perception might be at least a little bit subjective and—dare I say—unreliable. Hold your opinion of them with open hands and an open mind, and be willing to change it as you get to know them more. That's what you want from others, and it's what they want from you.

My point is simply that labeling someone as difficult, frustrating, or problematic is a choice you make. Beauty is in the eye of the beholder, they say—and so is complicated.

The nice thing about your stories and perceptions is that you can change them. If you can choose to define someone as complicated, you can also choose *not* to define them as complicated. You can work from a hypothesis of generosity rather than one of villainy.

What if you tried a different label, one that put a positive spin on their quirks rather than a negative one? After all, that's probably what they're doing about their own quirks when they look in the mirror. And it's what you hope other people do when your complications rub them the wrong way. Try reframing those things as hero behavior and see how it changes your perspective of them.

ARE THEY OR ARE THEY

combative	honest
indecisive	analytical
loud	passionate
disorganized	creative
weak	caring
proud	confident
rude	direct
a loner	lonely
old-fashioned	experienced
weird	brilliant

Remember also that two things can be true at the same time. They might be a little bit on both sides of those phrases. Leave space for them to grow on you, for them to become more than just, "Yeah, they're complicated."

Isn't that the case with all of us, though? Our strengths can become weaknesses from time to time, but they are still strengths.

No strength comes without a downside, and no weakness comes without an upside. That's exactly why we need diverse teams: to watch each other's backs, to carry each other's burdens, and to receive each other's gifts.

Learn to frame people's differences in terms of what they add to the team rather than what they take away. If they're the loud one, the thoughtful one, the pushy one, the stubborn one, or the fearful one in the group, appreciate what that adds to the team dynamic.

And by the way, leave room for growth. People can change, like the basketball player I mentioned earlier. We can't keep holding each other prisoner to a past version of themselves.

Maya Angelou famously said, "When someone shows you who they are, believe them the first time." I think that's true and wise in the context of not letting yourself be abused or taken advantage of, but the focus of that statement is on who they are *now*. Don't use it as a weapon to cancel people for the rest of their lives.

After all, haven't you changed over the last five years? What if someone held you hostage to who you were when you graduated, when you first started your job, or when you were trying to figure out brand-new technology? Maybe there's a person in your life who was complicated five years ago, but they've been working on themselves since then. You might need to update your internal Wikipedia page for that individual, just like you want them to update their entry for you.

If you want to get better at collaborating with complicated colleagues, try using the power of story to reframe them in a more generous way. It won't fix their flaws, but it will help you notice their strengths. That's the power of telling yourself a better story: it allows you to see the best in everyone and collaborate effectively with (nearly) anyone.

GO LOOKING FOR COMPLICATED

Once you start telling yourself a more generous, positive story about the people around you, something strange often happens. You start *wanting* these people to be in your life and on your team. I mentioned earlier that one reason you need to get better at working with complicated people is because of what they add to your life, and that's what I'm talking about here.

Once you've got your story straight, though, it's not a forced camaraderie. You aren't making your world more diverse because you have to. Instead, you realize how much you gain by inviting people into it who have radically different personalities, worldviews, and experiences. You go looking for complicated.

In 1891, a young man named William Wrigley Jr. moved to Chicago with $32 and a dream of making his fortune in business. He started out by selling soap. To encourage people to buy his product, he gave away free baking soda with every purchase. The baking soda quickly turned out to be more popular with his customers than the soap, though. So he pivoted and started selling baking soda. This time, as an incentive to buy his product, he gave away sticks of free chewing gum. Soon, he realized his chewing gum was more popular than his baking soda, so he switched it up again. He began selling chewing gum, in particular a kind of gum he mixed with mint leaf juice.

That's how Wrigley's chewing gum was born. Today, Wrigley Company is a worldwide name with over a dozen brands of gum—including the classic Doublemint—for sale in more than 140 countries.[14, 15]

Cleary, William Wrigley Jr. knew how to listen to his customers. But he also knew how to listen to and learn from the people he hired.

In an interview for a magazine article called "Spunk Never Cost a Man a Job Worth Having" (I love that title), Wrigley said he preferred an employee "with backbone" who would challenge his ideas and tell him if he thought he was wrong. He stated,

> **ONE OF THE BIGGEST** pests in business is the carbon copy—the fellow who always says: "Yes, Mr. Wrigley, you're absolutely right." Perhaps meaning: "Have it your own way, you old buzzard, what do I care!" Business is built by men who care—care enough to disagree, fight it out to a finish, get facts. When two men always agree, one of them is unnecessary.[16]

That last line is especially profound. If two people always think the same, respond the same, dream the same, design the same, and work the same . . . then they're redundant. They don't add anything to each other except an extra set of hands.

Extra hands are nice.

But extra brains are even better.

The problem with brains, though, is that they have a mind of their own. Literally. They have their own opinions. Their own way of doing things. Their own goals, fears, emotions, and logic.

If you're like me, you might sometimes wish you could clone yourself in order to get more done with less drama. After all, a clone wouldn't throw off your groove. You wouldn't fight with a clone. You wouldn't disagree with a clone. You wouldn't have to teach a clone the same thing three times. Neither of you would whistle at work or chew loudly or show up late or do anything else that got on the other person's last nerve. You'd work in perfect, blissful, fight-free harmony. Sounds amazing, right?

No.

A partnership of clones would likely result in an efficient, drama-free trajectory right off a cliff of mediocrity. You'd groove together and lose together. You and your uncomplicated clone would make the same mistakes. You'd fall for the same scams. You'd make the same wrong decisions. You'd have the same limited skill sets. You'd have the same gaps in your knowledge and experience.

Of course a clone would be easier to work with, but is easier the same as better?

That's rhetorical, but I'm going to answer it anyway. No, it's not.

WE NEED PEOPLE WHO

know things we've never learned

have failed at things we've never tried

question what we accept

overcome challenges we've never faced

value what we overlook

remember what we forget

see an opportunity where we see an obstacle

AND THEY NEED US FOR THE EXACT SAME REASONS.

You and I will always need people who are different than us because no human being contains the sum total of knowledge, experience, and talent in the universe.

This is a little easier said than done, of course. It sounds so noble and mature to say, "People who are different are a gift. You need them, and they need you. Go hug a complicated person." But when the rubber meets the road and the smelly stuff hits the fan, it can be really hard to see differences as a positive. You're going to have to challenge your own inner drive to simplify, avoid discomfort, and be in control.

Research into why we get along with some people better than others points to the fact that "we tend to hang out with people whose brains work like ours do."[17] We often click with individuals who process information and events in ways similar to ours. We see through a similar lens. It feels more "natural" to gravitate toward people who look, think, talk, and act like us.

After all, we click with people who are like us. We flow. We vibe. We get each other. We have the same sense of humor. Birds of a feather flock together, and brains of a feather do too.

While that can be a positive thing if you're building a friendship, it can be a negative one if you're building a business, as Mr. Wrigley understood. If you want to create a product or service that appeals to a wide variety of people, you need to build a wide variety of thought into its creation. Diversity can't be an afterthought. It's critical to invention and innovation.

Complicated people are valuable not despite their differences, but precisely because of them. Look past the prickliness and pokiness of their personalities and genuinely appreciate what they bring to the table. It's not enough to remain unruffled and unaffected by them. That's avoidance. You have to actively seek some of these people out. And you might need to put some of them on your team.

Differences, diversity, and disagreements protect you. They make your world bigger. They spark the kind of synergy and creativity that result in industry-shifting innovation and world-changing companies. We think we want simple. But simple is often the trap we fall into, while complicated is the gift we need.

Knowing which differences are deal-breakers, which are bothersome but tolerable, and which are genuinely beneficial is rarely obvious at first. You have to work at it.

The good news is that this work changes you for the better. It helps you adjust and expand your world.

That's a gift, my friend.

A bigger, more connected world is far more valuable than achieving inbox zero, hitting every KPI, or coming in under budget. Those things matter, but they are superficial metrics of success. What really matters is how well you are able to incorporate other people into your life. Especially the complicated ones.

This is more than just a set of actions, though. It's more than a checklist or a to-do list. It's a mentality. A lens. A way of thinking.

I call it a collaboration mindset, and it's what we're going to turn to next.

CHAPTER 5

COLLABORATION IS A MINDSET

As a loud and proud sneakerhead, I love to follow shoe news. I read blogs, follow social media accounts, listen to podcasts, and browse online resellers. I know the designers and the artists and the history behind them.

Often the coolest, most sought-after shoes aren't made by one company. Rather, they are a collab. Rapper Travis Scott and Nike, for example, have partnered to reinvent Air Force 1, Air Jordan 1, and many more. These shoes typically can be resold for many times over their retail price because people love them so much.

The thing that is unique about this kind of collab is that it's a partnership between two brands that blends the best of both of them. They work together to produce something neither could have done on their own.

In a collab, artists don't stop being themselves. They don't create a new artist name that erases their identities. They don't put one person in charge and make the other one obey their every whim. Without losing the essence of what makes them each unique, two strong, creative forces merge their voices and talents to create something new.

A similar dynamic can take place when it comes to working with complicated people. It starts with adopting a collaborative way of approaching your connection: a collaboration mindset.

A mindset is simply a specific way of thinking. It's a lens you see the world through. Merriam-Webster defines it as "a mental attitude or inclination."[18] Psychologist Dr. Gary Klein writes, "A *mindset* is a belief that orients the way we handle situations—the way we sort out what is going on and what we should do. Our mindsets help us spot opportunities, but they can also trap us in self-defeating cycles."[19]

What if you looked at your work less like a bunch of individuals pushing and pulling and struggling with each other—and more like a collab? What if you asked yourself, *What could we create together? How could we each bring our essence, our voice, and our point of view into this interaction and build something that is a blend of us all?*

The result just might be beautiful.

Sure, it's a little chaotic, ambiguous, and risky. Both the process and the product will be different than you might expect or prefer. But maybe their complicated contribution is exactly what you need to go to the next level.

Earlier I mentioned that in our research, we explored pain points and negative fallout from complicated people. We also asked questions from the other side, focusing on positive results that could come from more effective collaboration. We wanted them to dream, to imagine a workplace where they didn't just have to sweep conflict under the carpet or grit their teeth and keep smiling when a complicated person did the complicated stuff they do.

When we asked people to pick the top three things they thought would improve in their workplace if they were able to deal more effectively with complicated people, job satisfaction was at the top of the list, with 44% of people identifying this benefit. That was closely followed by increased productivity and higher morale (40%).[20] Other results included better communication, better employee retention, improved mental health, increased engagement, more focus, greater trust in the company, and increased innovation.

If you made a dream list of your own, it would probably look similar. The problem is that we tend to lose sight of the rewards of healthy collabs because one to five people are melting our minds and screwing up our plans. We can't see the forest for the complicated trees.

Take a step back for a minute and consider what might happen if you intentionally adopted a way of thinking that broke you out of cycles of frustration and hopelessness due to specific people at your job. What if you could go into your day excited about creating rather than nervous about clashing? What if you could choose cooperation over competition, trust over suspicion, communication over control, interaction over imposition? What if you tuned in to the other person's personality, pace, and preferences and tried to find ways to merge them with your own, rather than making them flash points that drive the two of you apart?

Changing your mindset makes all the difference. Remember, you can't change the other person, but you can change how you see them. And how you see them is how you'll treat them.

In order to understand this mindset, let's break it down by looking at four elements of healthy collaboration:

1. **SELF-AWARENESS ASKS,** "What is it like to be on the other side of me?"

2. **OWNERSHIP ASKS,** "What is my part to play?"

3. **CURIOSITY ASKS,** "What is it like to be you?"

4. **CONNECTION ASKS,** "What brings us together?"

These things are important no matter what kind of person you're working with, but they really shine when you're dealing with the complicated ones. Unfortunately, that also happens to be when they are the hardest to remember.

I. SELF-AWARENESS: WHAT IS IT LIKE TO BE ON THE OTHER SIDE OF ME?

When speaking, I often share a story about a ten-minute conversation I had with Hall of Fame basketball player Kobe Bryant that had a deep impact on me. After my speech concludes, when I'm talking with people who were in the audience, they often have follow-up questions. *What was Kobe like? Was he fierce? Was he intense? Did he try to play you one-on-one?*

I've gotten used to hearing the same general questions. But one time, after an event in Iowa, a leader asked me something I'd never been asked before: "Ryan, when you met Kobe, was he in a hurry? I'd imagine being on the other side of a busy guy like that would feel like he's in a hurry."

The question caught me by surprise, but my answer was simple and honest. "No, he wasn't. He was extremely present."

Ironically, the guy who was asking me that question had caught me outside, waiting for my Uber. So the person he was asking about Kobe being in a hurry . . . was actually in a hurry.

That moment made me rewind the tapes of interactions I've had with people all over the world. I found myself wondering how many people have been on the other side of me and felt like I was in a hurry. I began to notice that when I got off the stage and chatted with people, they started talking faster. They seemed to feel like they were on a shot clock with me and time was running out.

It was a blind spot that was hindering my connection with people. After a good dose of self-reflection and brutal honesty, I decided that in every interaction—even when I was literally in a hurry—I would attempt to slow down long enough to look someone in the eye and allow them—and me—to take a deep breath.

Self-awareness is really about asking yourself, *What's it like to be on the other side of me?* It can be defined as "the ability to take oneself as the object of attention and thought."[21] It describes your capacity to distance yourself from yourself in order to know yourself better. Don't expect to get better at working with complicated people unless you're willing to get better at understanding the person in the mirror.

When you become self-aware, you pay attention to how you show up in each situation. This goes beyond just noticing the words you say or the actions you take. It includes the deep-seated beliefs you bring to the table, the past traumas and victories that have shaped your emotional makeup, your worldview, your upbringing, your value system, and so much more. It also includes things as simple as recognizing when you're exhausted, stressed, hungry, or tired. Toddlers have very little self-awareness, obviously, but sometimes even grown adults would do well to be like toddlers and take a nap break or a snack break.

Self-awareness is crucial because in every interaction you have with complicated people, *you* are involved. You are the common denominator. This doesn't make you "the problem," but it does make you part of the solution, and that's good news. Learning to reflect on how you show up in complicated relationships is like unlocking a secret level or gaining a special power.

Calling someone complicated actually says as much about you as it does about them. Not in a bad way—in an informative way, if you use it as a springboard to dive deeper into yourself. Your reaction to challenging, difficult people can help you identify things such as:

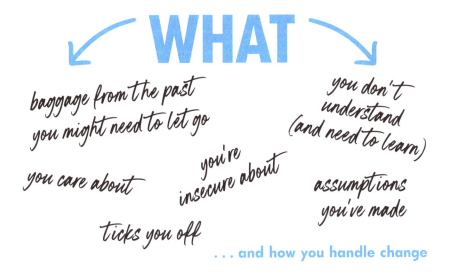

WHAT
- baggage from the past you might need to let go
- you care about
- you're insecure about
- ticks you off
- you don't understand (and need to learn)
- assumptions you've made

. . . and how you handle change

If a complicated person helps you understand a few of these things better, they are giving you a gift. It's a gift hidden inside an uncomfortable package, for sure, but if you can get past the box it comes in, that knowledge of self will help improve so many areas of your life, including how you show up in your friendships and with your family.

Better awareness of self leads to better awareness of others. It's hard to address someone else's problems if you're oblivious to your own. Yet that's what we often try to do, because it's easier to criticize than to self-reflect. So before you judge the complicated person down the hall, get to know the complicated person in the mirror.

Interestingly, when we work on ourselves first, we don't just see other people more clearly; we see them more compassionately. Often, by the time we're done reflecting on our own issues, we realize that at least a few of the other person's issues really aren't that big a deal. Some things can be overlooked. Others can be forgiven. And a few can even be embraced.

One of the things that can make us complicated is our power within the organization. If we're in a leadership role, whether formal or informal, self-awareness is especially important. It's all too easy to let power blind us to how other people perceive our interactions.

> **For example, one interesting detail that rose to the surface in our survey was that almost half (48%) of executives say they constantly or often experience a positive resolution to the challenges of working with complicated individuals. That sounds great . . . until you realize that managers report only 36% and employees a dismal 27%.**

Now, maybe these leaders are phenomenal at conflict resolution and team building. Maybe that's why they have their roles in the first place.

Or . . . maybe they are walking away from difficult interactions saying, "Solved! I took care of it! That worked out well!" while those with less power have a totally different view.

Either is possible. And that's why self-awareness matters.

Leaders who don't consider what their followers might think or feel can end up misjudging wins and losses and overestimating their leadership skills. Self-awareness as a leader means asking yourself, *Is my team as happy, safe, and unified as I think it is, or have they just learned how to say the right things so they don't lose their jobs?*

> **Interestingly, men reported a 35% resolution rate regarding the challenges of working with complicated individuals while women were significantly lower, at 28%. I doubt that means women are naturally worse at social interactions (data from other studies seems to say the opposite),[22] but rather that they tend to face more obstacles than men do in their pursuit of resolution.**

As a man in the workplace, this should make me reevaluate whether what I call "complicated" is influenced by gender stereotypes and whether I'm responding the same way to women as I do to men. I'd like to believe I am . . . but I can't just make that assumption.

Neither can you.

> **Age matters too. We were surprised to discover that those in the 18–29 age bracket reported the most success (40%, which still isn't high by any stretch of the imagination). That dropped steadily with each age range—all the way down to workers ages 60–65, who have a scary-low 14% success rate. The older people are, the less they feel their problems are being resolved.**

Besides roles, gender, and age, other factors also affected whether people felt their complicated-people problems were resolved. We found significant differences within industries, levels of education, political and religious beliefs, and more.

Alright, so what does all that mean for you? Simply that you need to constantly engage self-awareness. You should be asking yourself regularly, *Am I as effective as I think when it comes to dealing with complicated people, or are other people walking away with an entirely different view of what just happened?*

What's it like to be on the other side of you?

If you can answer that honestly and humbly, you'll be well on your way to better collaboration.

2. OWNERSHIP: WHAT IS MY PART TO PLAY?

I have two small boys, and their relationship is . . . complicated. They love each other, but they also argue way too much and way too loudly—especially when I'm trying to get work done in my office down the hall.

Naturally, whenever I hear them arguing about something and I try to help them figure things out, they both act like they're the victim in the fight. It's always "his" fault. As a parent, I know it takes two kids to make that kind of noise. But as long as they're pointing fingers at each other, they'll never resolve the conflict and, more importantly, never learn and grow.

Something similar holds true in many workplace conflicts. No matter what complicated person you're dealing with, at least some of the responsibility for your workday experiences and interpersonal relationships probably lies with you.

That's a good thing. It means you can improve the situation—even if it's just a little—by owning your role in the situation.

It might be true that "they started it," to quote one of my kids' favorite lines, but you have a choice about how to respond. You can't control the other person's actions, but you can always control your reactions. You don't have to make things even more complicated by overreacting to them.

Ownership is about figuring out what you can actually change. What is under your control and what is not? What is your responsibility right here, right now?

If you believe you can't change anything, learn anything, or fix anything, then your current situation can't improve. You're a prisoner of someone else's choices.

But it's a prison of your own making.

Because there are always things you can do. You just have to start with yourself. The question to ask in any messy, complex relationship, therefore, is: "What is my part to play?"

Author and pastor Steven Furtick has this mantra: "I'm not stuck unless I stop."[23] Without discounting your pain, I want to encourage you to not see yourself as stuck. Yes, you're facing an obstacle, but you are only stuck if you choose to stop, because that's the moment when you relinquish your autonomy.

Is there something, anything, no matter how small, that you could do? That's ownership. It's being willing to keep moving and keep trying, even when you're giving 98% and the other person is only giving 2%. Working with complicated people isn't fun or fair. The other person probably should change, and in a perfect world, they would. But this isn't a perfect world. It's a complicated one. So even if you can't make the collaboration perfect, can you at least make it better?

Now, as I mentioned before, a collab doesn't mean changing yourself so much that you lose yourself. This book isn't called *How to Be a Chameleon Around Complicated People.* You don't need to change who you are on the inside, put on a façade, or go to ridiculous extremes just to meet the whims of fickle, frustrating, immature people.

All I'm saying is that when you focus on what is within your control, hope will rise and creativity will kick in.

In the context of complicated people, ask yourself,

WHAT AM I RESPONSIBLE FOR HERE?

Then ask a follow-up question:

AM I MANAGING THAT RESPONSIBILITY TO THE BEST OF MY ABILITY?

3. CURIOSITY: WHAT IS IT LIKE TO BE YOU?

I'm going to give you a question I believe can help you move toward understanding all the complicated people you work with. You can ask yourself this question about them, or if the moment is right and you're feeling brave, you can ask them directly:

What is it like to be you?

By asking this, you are building a bridge and crossing into their world. Instead of just hanging out in your own head, you're actually getting into someone else's.

It's easy to make snap judgments about someone's motivations or intentions based on surface impressions, but when you step into what it's like to be them and truly seek to understand, you create an environment where work is a little less complicated and teamwork can thrive. Curiosity is always a better response than frustration, so reach for this question at the first sign of conflict or confusion. For example:

- **I wonder what going through the hiring process here was like for you.**

- **I'm curious about the emotions you navigate being the only remote member of our team.**

- **I wonder what extra pressures and expectations you deal with as the only woman on the board.**

- **I'd love to know how you manage your work-life balance given the demands of this job.**

- **I can only imagine the pressure you might feel being the youngest team lead here.**

- **Given the rapid pace of our industry, I'm curious how it feels to be constantly adapting to new technologies.**

This is about humanizing people. If you reduce them to a label, if you say they are too difficult to work with, too stubborn, too different, too weird, too stuck in their ways, too old or too young, too Boomer or too Millennial, then learning and growth get shut down, connections get shut off, and people get shut out.

What's it like to be you? is a dangerous question. It might spark compassion. It might build the relationship. It might push you to study and learn. It might even make things more complicated, but in a good way, because it will reveal that person's humanity and make it harder to judge them and discard them.

What I've found is that people get less complicated the more you get to know them. They get more nuanced, but less complicated. There's a difference between those words, and it can be the difference between drawing someone close and pushing them away.

The better you understand the layers that make up any given person, the easier it is to see past their prickliness and value what lies underneath. First impressions never tell the whole story. Beneath their grumpiness, their perfectionism, their language barrier, or their irritating habit of watching YouTube videos at full volume lies a complex, nuanced individual.

It's a strategy and a trait that can defuse tense situations and disarm combative people. It will carry you closer to the other person, not farther from them. It will help you meet in the middle, rather than digging trenches and dying on opposite hills.

Curiosity is a superpower that is available to anyone.

CURIOSITY IS A SUPERPOWER THAT IS AVAILABLE TO ANYONE.

Curiosity will help you understand the person better, and understanding can change everything. For instance, I was chatting with an executive one time, and he told me one of his top sales leaders had been struggling recently. So he spoke with him, and he found out his wife had recently left him and taken the kids. That knowledge changed this executive's perspective on his employee.

Being curious about people is a subset of curiosity about the world around you, which is a trait we should all have. Keep learning. Keep growing. Keep Googling. Keep ChatGPT'ing, if that's a word. Get comfortable with the reality of your ignorance. Learn to say things like, "I don't know," or "What do you think?" or "What am I missing here?" or "Help me see your point of view."

Think of your brain as a library. The more knowledge stored there, the more you can pull from to connect with others. Read books, listen to podcasts, take online courses, watch documentaries, go to conferences. Go out for coffee with someone and take notes on what they're learning. You'd be surprised what you'll hear when you ask people, "What have you been learning lately?" Grow your knowledge, and you'll grow your connections.

Two words of caution here. First, none of us can fully figure our own complicated selves out, which means we shouldn't arrogantly assume we have other people totally figured out either. Do your best to understand where people are coming from, but hold your conclusions in an open hand. Be willing to change them again and again as you get to know the person better.

Second, you don't need to decide if everything about the other person is "right" or "wrong." Obviously, you can and should identify genuinely abusive or illegal behavior, but you don't have to judge every quirk, quality, and characteristic you come across. Let people be loud without saying they're "too loud." Let them be spontaneous without calling them "too spontaneous." Let them be quiet, cautious, loud, worried, detail-oriented, casual, or whatever else they might be without assuming they're too much of something. Often the word *too* simply means they deviate from your expectations, not from some universal standard.

And of course, they're probably looking at you and saying you are "too . . . " but in the opposite direction.

Everyone has their issues, including you and me. Everyone's a fixer-upper. Are you going to resent them or strive to understand them? Are you going to judge people or listen to them, learn about them, and build bridges to them?

The next time you find your inner temperature reaching a boiling point with someone, try asking: "What's it like to be you?"

THEN SEE WHERE YOUR CURIOSITY LEADS YOU.

4. CONNECTION: WHAT BRINGS US TOGETHER?

The final component of a collaboration mindset is connection. Self-awareness, ownership, and curiosity are all meant to lead you here, to the place where you establish a meaningful, productive working relationship with someone you might otherwise have avoided entirely.

This is where the magic happens.

Connections between people are like sparks of electricity that jump between two neurons in the human brain. Your brain is an engineering marvel. It has around eighty-six billion neurons. Each of these neurons has multiple connections with other neurons—anywhere from a few of them to hundreds of thousands.[24] And yet, the whole thing is incredibly efficient, using less power than a lightbulb.[25]

Without the sparks, there's no magic. No movement. Just a lot of neurons chilling side by side and never getting anything done.

What if we looked at our workplace less as a loose collection of random people and more like an interconnected brain? What if we realized that the sparks that fly between us are what makes things happen? That the frequency and quality of our connections is what turns a roomful of individuals into an unstoppable team?

The problem is that we often tend to downplay connections and hyperfocus on individuals. We assume that to get better results, either the people on our team need to get better, we need to get better people on our team, or both. But what if the answer lies not only in improving *individuals* but also in improving the *connections* between those individuals?

As it turns out, research shows these connections are incredibly important—so much so, in fact, that the connection between two people can matter as much or more as the individual intelligence of each one.

In 2010, researchers conducted two studies to see if they could discover a "collective intelligence" factor that would predict which groups would tend to perform best regardless of the task at hand. In other words, can teams be "smart"? Can you build a team that will be able to tackle a variety of jobs and consistently have good results? And if so, what factors make one team smarter than another?

They concluded that teams can, in fact, have a collective intelligence, which they called a "c factor."[26] They also came to some interesting conclusions about what exactly makes a team intelligent.

First, here's what they *didn't* find: "Many of the factors one might have expected to predict group performance—such as group cohesion, motivation, and satisfaction—did not."

That's not to say these things are unimportant. Of course you want teams that are unified, energized, and satisfied. But those were not the specific things that made a consistent, measurable difference in how smart a particular team proved to be.

It gets more interesting. The researchers determined, "This 'c factor' is not strongly correlated with the average or maximum individual intelligence of group members." They found that average intelligence and maximum intelligence were moderately correlated, but not strongly correlated.

What does that mean for those of us who don't speak PhD? It means that it didn't matter all that much whether or not the team members were exceptionally smart or had a particularly brainy person on their team. While those factors helped a little, they didn't make or break the team, and they didn't do that great of a job predicting how well these teams were going to perform in different tasks.

Conventional wisdom says if you assemble the brightest minds in a room, you automatically set yourself up for success. You'll get the smartest ideas, greatest solutions, and best results. But these studies did not back that assumption up.

What the researchers did find is even more fascinating. Out of the different factors they tested for, they concluded that the collective intelligence of the teams in the study was primarily related to three things: "the average social sensitivity of group members, the equality in distribution of conversational turn-taking, and the proportion of females in the group."

In other words, how smart your group is, according to these studies, will be influenced significantly by:

how *socially sensitive your team members are, meaning you are able to read and respond to each other's social cues;*

whether *everyone gets a turn to talk, which seems like basic manners but is often not the case in group settings; and*

whether *many women are on the team.*

Based on further analysis, they concluded the gender factor was due primarily to the fact that women consistently scored higher than men in the social sensitivity area, and that of the three factors, social sensitivity was the most important.

Do you see how these findings point to connection? A team's ability to read each other, to understand each other, and to listen and talk things out like civilized human beings is foundational to their "smartness." (And in case you missed it, women tend to be better at that than men, which is one of many reasons we need diverse teams.)

"Getting the right people on the bus" matters, as we often say. But these people have to be able to get along. They need to be able to connect and collaborate. If they can't, they're not the right people after all. The ability to create and sustain high-quality connections is the secret ingredient that takes teams to the next level. I think success is often less about superheroes and more about synergy. It's less about the parts and more about the whole.

So sure, try to put awesome people on a team. But invest just as much energy into making sure those awesome people know how to get along and work together. They have to function like a brain, with multiple synapses firing all over the place, working together for a common goal. They have to be able to communicate and collaborate, to interreact and intersect, to vibe together and jibe together, to move as one and groove as one.

What does this mean for your quest to collaborate with complicated? It means that instead of hyperfixating or hyperventilating about people's quirks, focus on where and how you can connect. Ask, "What brings us together? Where do we intersect? Where do we engage?" Then work on making those connections as strong as possible.

In their book *Flock Not Clock,* authors and researchers Derek and Laura Cabrera argue that companies are complex, always-adapting systems that behave more like a flock of birds or a school of fish than predictable, controllable systems. Because we live and work in a constantly changing world made up of perpetually moving parts, what matters most is how well people are able to stay connected to everyone else in this mad dance called humanity. The Cabreras write, "The people with the most and highest quality relationships are the most connected, and therefore the most influential in the system."[27]

Connection is the currency of the workplace. Org charts don't always tell the whole story because where the power truly lies is with the people who are the best at building and maintaining relationships with others, including ones who are wildly different from them (a.k.a. "the complicated ones"). These individuals might not have the title or the paycheck or the corner office, but they have clout. They have pull. People seek them out and listen to them and follow them. Why? Because they invest in building connections with people, and connections matter most.

In a world that runs on connection, look for the things that bring you and other people together. Invest in building greater quality and quantity of interactions. Sure, it's messy and chaotic at times, but it will make you more valuable, more effective, and more secure.

It should be obvious that these four elements of a collaboration mindset—self-awareness, ownership, curiosity, and connection—are not destinations you arrive at. They are more like the vehicles you drive to get where you want to go, which is collaboration.

This entire collaborating-with-complicated-people thing is a work in progress because humans are a work in progress, and you and I are both very much human. That means you need to keep asking yourself these same four questions, every chance you get, in any situation you find yourself in, no matter who you're dealing with or how complicated they turn out to be:

- **"What is it like to be on the other side of me?" (self-awareness)**

- **"What is my part to play?" (ownership)**

- **"What is it like to be you?" (curiosity)**

- **"What brings us together?" (connection)**

Whether you're a rapper designing shoes with Nike or a manager trying to hit your end-of-quarter goals, having a collaboration mindset is the key to working well with other people. It is what enables you to build bridges rather than walls and draw people closer rather than push them away.

Bridge-building is the art we're going to turn to next. In order to span the gaps that separate us from complicated colleagues and to establish the connections that are so vital to collaboration, we need to hone five specific skills.

Together, I call these People Qs.

CHAPTER 6

PEOPLE Qs

I've taken a lot of personality assessments in my career. I'm an ENTJ on the Myers-Briggs Type Indicator. I'm an "I" type in the DISC assessment. I'm the color Red according to the Taylor Hartman Color Code. I'm a number 3 on the Enneagram. According to my StrengthsFinder results, my strengths are communication, command, harmony, adaptability, and ideation. And according to those random and peculiar online quizzes, if I were a Marvel character, I'd be Black Panther, and my Harry Potter house would be Gryffindor.

Personality is only one part of who we are, though. It gets even more complex when you stir into the pot other concepts used to describe people: things like intelligence types, learning styles, love languages, and attachment styles. And it gets still more dizzying when you consider the lifetime of unique experiences that have shaped each of us differently.

Once you start mixing and matching different ways of categorizing people, you realize there's an infinite combination of humans walking around out there in the wild. It's not just our fingerprints that are unique, but everything about us. No two people are alike.

And yet, somehow we're supposed to be able to work with them all.

That is low-key terrifying because we often don't have a voice or a vote regarding the people we work with. We're pretty much stuck with anyone who has been assigned to our workspace by the powers that be. And yet, our productivity, prosperity, and sanity hang on whether we can figure out how to work with these weirdos. (And remember that at least a couple of them are thinking the same thing about you.)

Because the people you work with are infinitely complex, you need to be able to figure them out in real time, on a case-by-case basis. You can't simply memorize four DISC types or twenty-seven Enneagram combinations and assume you now have absolute knowledge of all humanity. You have to dig a lot deeper than that.

In order to work effectively with people—especially the complicated ones—you need to become a people person.

I don't necessarily mean you have to become an extrovert. You don't have to host cocktail parties or take up karaoke. Relax. I'm an introvert too. I feel your pain every time the holiday season rolls around. By January 2, I don't want to socialize again until at least spring break.

By people person, I simply mean you must become a student of people. An expert in humans. A teachable, growing individual who is curious about the nuances and flavors of humanity rather than feeling intimidated by them.

You can't fit people into tidy little boxes that will always predict their behavior, but you can get closer to understanding them if you're willing to work at it a little. And often, closer is all you need to take your work relationship from difficult to dynamic.

In this chapter, we're going to explore five "People Qs," which are metrics or skills that will move you one step closer to the people you work with. The letter Q stands for quotient, and it was made famous by the granddaddy of them all: IQ, or *intelligence quotient*, which attempts to measure and rank human intelligence. Since IQ came on the scene over one hundred years ago, numerous other Qs have popped up to evaluate other competencies as well.

Remember, though, we want to know how to collaborate with people—especially the prickly, cranky, wonky ones. That's why I call these People Qs, and it's why I'm framing them as connections rather than just competencies. I want to explore how you can get better at using these concepts to build bridges that reach (nearly) anyone.

First up: the OG metric, the one people love to hate (unless they score high on it, in which case they tend to think it's all that matters). I'm talking, of course, about IQ.

I. IQ CONNECTION: INTELLIGENCE AND KNOWLEDGE

Not long ago, I was invited to speak at a hair and makeup convention. Eight hundred experts in hair and makeup were going to listen to a dude with no makeup and short hair give a keynote address.

It was . . . complicated. Not because anyone was bad or malicious, but because I was far away from them on a knowledge level, and I needed to build a bridge.

I wasn't there to give them tips on conditioners or contouring, of course. I was speaking about failure and success, and those are universal topics. But I knew gaining their trust would be an uphill battle simply because I didn't speak their language.

So I spent some time learning it. I did some research on hair and makeup so I wouldn't be walking into that speech like a total newbie. I learned about bobs, bangs, undercuts, and feathering. I read about flat irons, curling irons, and every kind of brush you can imagine. I added words like blending, baking, and strobing to my vocabulary.

It wasn't a lot, but it was enough to crack a couple of jokes, mention a few pain points, and in general build a bridge of shared vocabulary and knowledge. It also gave me a window into their world. I found my respect for their professionalism growing with everything I learned.

I make a habit of researching new "languages" because I've found that ignorance undermines connection and credibility, and that ruins communication. So today, I speak many languages. Not fluently, but enough to relate effectively. I speak football, even though I've never tackled anyone and getting pummeled by a three-hundred-pound linebacker sounds like hell. I speak automotive, even though I've never flushed a radiator (what does that even mean?), and I have zero desire to try. I speak church, tech ops, farming, finance, retail, and healthcare. I speak Boomer and Gen Z. I speak executive, employee, entrepreneur, and solopreneur.

I choose to because my connection depends on it.

And so does yours.

If you're going to work effectively with complicated people, you'll need to become multilingual. You'll need to cross the knowledge gap by using the three most important pounds in your body: those eighty-six billion neurons that make up your brain.

I call this the IQ connection.

I doubt any other Q in our list has been studied as deeply or criticized as loudly as IQ. This isn't just because it's been around for so long, but because IQ tests are notoriously limited in what they can actually measure. They basically tell you how good you are at pattern recognition, logical thinking, and other related cognitive abilities compared to everyone else . . . and that's about it. Whether that translates into real-world success depends on many other factors.

Howard Gardner is a revered psychologist and education expert who is best known for his theory of multiple intelligences. Gardner believes there are at least eight "intelligences," or ways of being smart, and IQ tests address only two of them. In an interview with Big Think, he stated, "It's great to have language and logical intelligence because most tests really focus on that. And if you do well in those tests, as long as you stay in school, you think you're smart. But if you ever walk out into Broadway or a highway or into the woods or into a farm, you then find out that other intelligences are at least as important."[28]

You probably experienced this back in high school. The nerds were brain smart. The jocks were sports smart. The popular kids were people smart. Other kids were music smart, art smart, tech smart, science smart, nature smart, or emotions smart.

People are smart, and they know it. In one US survey, 65% of people agreed with the statement, "I am more intelligent than the average person."[29] In other words, almost two-thirds of people think they are above average when it comes to brains. That's not possible, though.

Or is it?

I laughed at that statistic at first, but then I started thinking. I suspect those 65% were rating their own specific type of intelligence. That's valid, in my humble opinion. For me, the IQ connection includes all forms of "smart," even if they wouldn't show up on your average IQ test.

The real question, though, isn't whether you are smart or not (you are) or in what way you are smart (hopefully you know that). It's this:

Can you use your smarts to connect to other people?

Especially the complicated ones?

Do you understand their world? Can you speak their language? Can you value their way of being intelligent? Are you actively attempting to learn what you need to know so you can collaborate better? Are you curious, are you a student, are you growing? Can you use information and understanding as a point of connection?

Unfortunately, many people are unwilling to engage their brainpower to build connections. They know what they know, and that's enough, they think.

It's not that their *IQ* is low. They might be brilliant individuals. But their *IQ connection* is low. They're not using their brains to build bridges. They're content to stay on their little knowledge islands, isolated and alienated by a lack of mental connection.

The IQ connection, then, is about using your intelligence––whatever kind you happen to have––to collaborate more effectively with the people around you. You improve your IQ connection by taking the initiative to cross the knowledge gap.

A friend of mine told me about how, years ago, his two kids were going through a stage where they fought a lot, mostly because the younger one had gotten old enough to know what she wanted and to stand up for herself, and her older brother, a middle schooler, wasn't used to that. The brother told his dad how frustrated he was that his sister was "always so stubborn and unreasonable."

My friend said, "You're a smart guy. Stop getting mad at her and figure out how to work with her." He saw the lightbulb turn on in his son's brain. Apparently, he had never considered using negotiation skills with his sister. So he started looking for ways to make things a win-win rather than just demanding that she do what he wanted. Fights went down and cooperation went up. The story gave me hope for my two boys, both under ten, whose negotiation skills are nonexistent at this point.

This isn't just a skill for sibling rivalries; it's a skill for life. You are a smart person. Don't get mad, frustrated, or hopeless. Figure out strategies to connect, to make things a win-win, to motivate people rather than berating them.

If you're one of the 65% who are smarter than average, prove it by connecting with people who think differently than you. Don't just complain about their lack of knowledge, their stubbornness, or their unreasonableness. Use your brain to build a bridge. Learn their language instead of demanding they learn yours.

As you begin to build a knowledge bridge, look for places where you connect. You'll never be exactly the same as anyone else, but you will share at least something in common. Probably quite a few things, if you dig around long enough.

Instead of fixating on the disconnect, focus on the places your dreams, talents, knowledge, relationships, or even hobbies intersect with theirs. Start there. Build rapport and trust, then move outward into more unfamiliar or awkward territory.

2. EQ CONNECTION: EMOTIONS AND FEELINGS

Next up: your EQ connection. This refers to your *emotional intelligence.* How aware are you of the emotions that you and those around you are experiencing, and how well can you manage those emotions?[30]

This isn't just for the touchy-feely empath types who cry over greeting card commercials. We all have emotions, and often an emotional connection with someone can be far more powerful than an intellectual one.

Emotions encompass a vast range of human experiences. Psychologists have attempted to list, define, and categorize them, but they defy easy organization. There are the obvious ones such as happiness, sadness, love, anger, and fear, but they are just the tip of the emotional iceberg. Think about:

nostalgia	loneliness
gratitude	trust
vulnerability	awe
curiosity	humiliation
frustration	worry
shock	compassion
envy	confusion
sympathy	despair
disappointment	melancholy
contempt	relief
bravery	embarrassment
hope	anticipation
bitterness	satisfaction
panic	shame
guilt	terror
pride	**. . . just to name a few.**

It's not hard to see how important emotional intelligence is when it comes to dealing with complicated people. These are the people who make our blood boil, who get us frustrated, angry, resentful, hopeless, and depressed. If we are going to collaborate with them effectively, we need to get better at identifying what is happening emotionally and bringing it under control.

One person I interviewed for this book is the general manager at a fitness club. She mentioned that clients often arrive amped up on pre-workout drinks and in a hurry to jump into their routine. They're ready to lift something, chase something, or punch something. If they run into a minor setback, such as a problem with their membership status, they can go from zero to pissed off in two seconds flat. Then they tear into whichever poor employee is tasked with helping them. The GM told me she often has to sit with new employees in her office and walk them through the process of handling their own emotions after they just got chewed out by a caffeine-crazed gym rat.

Think about all the levels of emotional intelligence at work here. First, you have the club member. They're losing their mind over a relatively minor issue, but they don't realize how dramatic they're being in the moment. The issue is bigger than life to them because their heart rate has been artificially enhanced by whatever mysterious potion they guzzled on their way to the gym. They need more EQ for sure, but they're not even thinking about that.

Then you have the employee, who is being paid to make the workout experience a positive one . . . but who also has emotions and a life of their own. They don't unplug their feelings when they put on a uniform. They are already facing their fair share of craziness in their personal lives, and now they have to be the emotional punching bag for someone else. That's not easy for anyone.

Finally, you have the GM. She gets the unenviable job of calming down her customers while also keeping her staff sane and smiling. Oh yeah, and she has to do this while also managing her own emotions, because GMs are people too.

IT'S COMPLICATED!

BUT IT'S NOT IMPOSSIBLE.

AND

ACTUALLY, IT'S ESSENTIAL.

We have to learn to give emotions their place. No more, no less. Emotions spice up your life, but they don't run it. They influence your decisions, but they don't make them for you. Sometimes we forget this, and in the name of "validating our feelings," we end up abdicating control to them. That's not any healthier than stifling them would be.

On the other hand, while emotions don't belong behind the steering wheel, they don't deserve to be locked in the trunk either. So move them to the passenger seat. They're a little bit like your spouse or significant other: fun to have on a road trip, helpful, spicy, and with a tendency to overreact when they think you don't see the brake lights ahead. Listen to them, but not so much that you panic and end up in a ditch.

If you don't get the better of your emotions, they'll get the better of you—usually at the worst possible time. Do what you need to do to improve in this area. Go to therapy. Download a meditation app. Get more sleep at night. Keep granola bars at your desk so your blood sugar doesn't get too low. Whatever it takes, develop emotional intelligence and use it to connect with other people, especially the ones who tend to trigger those emotions the quickest—the complicated people.

The good news is that while emotions handled the wrong way can blow up a relationship, emotions handled the right way can strengthen it.

THAT'S THE POWER OF THE EQ CONNECTION.

- **If you can figure out the pain, fear, or hurt behind someone's actions, you'll be able to engage more thoughtfully with them.**

- **If you can refuse to let your emotions get triggered too easily, you'll be able to let potential offenses wash off you and move into collaboration.**

- **If you can be aware of the ebb and flow of emotions during a high-stress project, you'll know when to take a break and when to give people grace.**

- **If you can listen without judgment when someone vents, you'll gain their trust to help them move forward when they've finished expressing themselves.**

Emotions are a normal part of being human, which means they should be a normal part of working together. Usually, emotions are trying to tell you something, and you should listen. Don't be too quick to judge or condemn yourself or anyone else just because tensions are running high in the room. Instead, lean in, validate other people's emotions—as well as your own—and learn what you can.

When people express emotions, even if they do it poorly, they are offering you a connection point. You just have to understand what they are feeling. Are they scared of change? Instead of dismissing their concern, listen to it and take it seriously. Are they insecure about their role? Reassure them that they bring something invaluable to the table.

You can even stop the conversation or meeting and address the emotional elephant in the room: "There are obviously some strong feelings about this topic. Why don't we take a moment and talk about why that is?" Instantly the conversation will go deeper than whatever you're arguing about, and you'll start discussing fears, pain, dreams, and values.

The beautiful thing is that if you can walk through those conversations and emotions together, you'll usually come out closer than ever, bonded through shared experiences and vulnerability.

Don't ignore, vilify, resent, or get steamrolled by emotions. Instead, identify them, manage them, and use them to build human bridges with even the most complicated people.

3. AQ CONNECTION: ADAPTABILITY AND CHANGE

The third Q, *adaptability quotient*, can be described as "an individual's ability to adjust to change in real time."[31] This is about how well someone navigates the constantly shifting and often chaotic world we live and work in. While the concept of an adaptability quotient isn't as widespread or studied as IQ and EQ, it's a helpful way to visualize this idea of dealing with change.

- **Are you willing to adjust your expectations and strategies?**

- **Can you pivot quickly when something doesn't work?**

- **Are you able to keep your head in times of ambiguity or upheaval?**

- **Can you experiment and iterate as needed?**

Probably all of us know someone who is not great at this. When plans don't work out, they panic. When faced with ambiguity, they freeze. When the answer is uncertain, they become stressed and anguished. When change comes, they spend most of their energy mourning the good old days instead of embracing the present day.

If we're honest, we've probably had those reactions a few times ourselves. It's human nature to be cautious of change, if not outright resistant to it. It's easy to become so risk-averse that you become change-averse, and those are two entirely different things.

One of the C-suite leaders I interviewed, an insurance industry executive, mentioned what he called CAVE people. The acronym stands for Citizens Against Virtually Everything. These are the ones who don't care what the plan, idea, or change is—they already know it's bad. They don't even need to hear it before they make up their mind.

I'm not a CAVE person, but I've been in CAVE moods before. I've had CAVE reactions to specific situations, and I didn't like it. I don't want to think that way, act that way, or talk that way. Nothing good comes from chronically bad attitudes, and negative mindsets don't lead to positive results.

We need to be able to adapt. In real time. On the fly. Again and again and again.

"In a world of constant change, the spoils go to the nimble," write business consultants Martin Reeves and Mike Deimler in their *Harvard Business Review* article "Adaptability: The New Competitive Advantage." They make the observation that we live in a time of risk and instability, which means traditional strategies such as long-term planning and strict hierarchies of power don't necessarily work. They state, "Traditional approaches to strategy—though often seen as the answer to change and uncertainty—actually assume a relatively stable and predictable world." They argue that "instead of being really good at doing some particular thing, companies must be really good at learning how to do new things."[32]

In other words, adaptability is a skill that will come in handy in a changing world, both for individuals and for companies.

It should be obvious how important a healthy AQ can be when you're working with complicated people. In your quest to collaborate more effectively with people who are very different from you, you're going to have to pivot. You're going to have to experiment, learn, change, and grow.

A high AQ connection means you can build a higher quantity and quality of bridges because you're not limited to just "one type" of person, and you don't need everyone to meet your expectations before you can start working together.

There is a limit to this. I'm not suggesting you bend over backward to accommodate every whim or whine from a complicated colleague. You're not trying to be:

- **A pushover, unable to stand up for anything**

- **A chameleon, constantly changing your behavior to fit in**

- **A manipulator, playing a part just to get what you want**

- **A liar, telling people what they want to hear**

- **A victim, allowing abuse or bullying in the name of getting the job done**

You're trying to be an effective team player. To do so, you have to be skilled and knowledgeable enough to work with a wide variety of people. You need to be clever and quick enough to adjust on the fly when someone drops the ball or needs some help. You must be ego-free enough to adjust some of your preferences or habits to merge more effectively with those around you. Adaptability is not a sign of weakness. It's a sign of maturity.

What does an AQ connection look like in real life? It all depends on the gaps you need to fill.

You know your team. Does one of them struggle with tech? You might want to explain something in more detail. Is someone chronically late to the office? Consider scheduling crucial meetings for nine o'clock instead of eight, just in case. Is another person hotheaded and easily ticked off? Try to break bad news diplomatically, then give them space to cool off.

An AQ connection also includes being aware of how other people are trying (or struggling) to adapt. Is your boss requiring people to return to the office? Are there rumors of a merger? Is your company rolling out a new software solution? Are you now outsourcing a service you've previously done in-house? Are you moving your offices to a new location? Are retirement plans changing?

Some of those things could be hugely important to you, and some might not matter at all. But they all matter to someone. After any announcement of change, somebody somewhere is probably freaking out a little, and it's not necessarily because they're dramatic. Maybe their resistance to change isn't due to stubbornness but to desperation.

Depending on your season of life and specific circumstances, what is good for you might be difficult for someone else, and what is difficult for you might be catastrophic for them. For you, new software might mean a bit of a learning curve, but for them, it might be a nearly insurmountable barrier that could cause them to fall behind and fade into irrelevance (or at least that's what they're afraid will happen). For you, a merger might mean reduced hours or even losing your job. But for them, it might mean losing not only a job but also the medical insurance their spouse or kids rely on.

Of course you wish complicated people would be simpler, but if you can't change them, try to adapt to them. A little flexibility goes a long way toward teamwork and peace.

Your ego might not like this, by the way, but ego isn't always the voice you should listen to. It will tell you to defend yourself, to prove something, to make them pay, to have the last petty word, to win pointless arguments, and to die on dumb hills.

If the other person is truly and consistently complicated, you will probably have to take a stand once in a while. Save that for the situations that really matter. The rest of the time, tell your ego to chill, then take the high road. Be the bigger person. Even if the complicated person doesn't notice, other people will; and in the long run, your adaptability and maturity will carry you further than cat-and-dog fights will.

Your connections with other humans will always be dynamic, unique, living things. Learn to adapt and adjust as needed to keep those connections flourishing.

4. TO CONNECTION: TECHNOLOGY AND INNOVATION

In the ever-evolving landscape of the workplace, technology has probably taken the most massive leaps of all.

If you were part of the workforce in the 1980s, you experienced the dawn of the "digital coworker." Computers were ugly, bulky, and nearly as big as people, and though they didn't gossip around the water cooler, they quickly replaced a lot of other human functions. Efficiency became king, and change became the norm.

Fast-forward to the 1990s, the decade of the Internet revolution. Hello, World Wide Web! Email became the new office memo. Online tools weren't just about faster communication; they were about broader connections stretching beyond cubicle walls. This was also the decade of pagers. At the ripe old age of eight, I knew two types of people who wore pagers: doctors and my brothers. I idolized both, and I dreamed of one day being successful enough to own a pager.

Enter the 2000s, the era of the "smart" revolution. The workplace got a lot smarter and smaller thanks to devices such as the iconic BlackBerry. I had a Sidekick from T-Mobile. If you don't know what that is, just imagine an iPhone that has a keyboard that slides out from the back and makes you think you're incredibly cool. We learned to carry our offices in our pockets. We began to understand the power of instant messaging for rapid responses and, probably more importantly, for building rapport in digital shorthand.

Then came the rising empires of social media and online networking tools in the 2010s. Social media wasn't just for cat videos anymore. LinkedIn, Slack, Microsoft Teams, and other platforms transformed how organizations could connect and collaborate. The art of "DM diplomacy" became as crucial as boardroom negotiations.

The 2020s started out with a curveball: the pandemic. Practically overnight, Zoom became our new best friend (or frenemy, depending on the strength of your Wi-Fi signal). Virtual meetings broke down physical barriers while introducing new ones, such as trying to read body language through pixels and screens. Then AI erupted on the scene, first as a buzzword, and then suddenly as a coworker. From automated customer service to voice cloning, AI is reshaping our understanding of productivity, creativity, and even empathy in the workplace.

In a work environment, technology isn't only about shiny gadgets or the newest fads, though those can be fun. It's also about understanding and leveraging new tools to work more effectively. That makes your *technological skill set,* or your TQ, as it's sometimes called, a key factor in your success over time.

Of course, this is a moving target, no matter how savvy you are, precisely because the world changes so quickly. Whether you consider yourself computer-illiterate or a technology god, you will still need to grow and change over time. We all will.

So, what is a TQ connection? It's about how well you use technology to collaborate with other people. Whether you're decoding an emoji-filled message from a Millennial team member or navigating a Zoom call with a tech-challenged boss, your TQ connection is about using technology to communicate better, understand deeper, and connect more effectively on a human level.

When it comes to TQ, there are two main types of complicated people. In the interest of humility, keep this in mind: if one of the two groups I'm about to describe is clearly "the problem" in your mind . . . then you might be in the other group, at least in the eyes of the people you see as the problem.

First, some people are complicated because *they can't (or won't) "keep up with the times" by adopting new technology.*

During the pandemic, you might have seen the viral video of an older lawyer who logged into a Zoom call with a judge and accidentally had a kitten face filter turned on. He showed up to a formal court hearing as an adorable but frustrated feline. His desperate plea to the judge, "I'm here live. I'm not a cat," became an instant Internet sensation.[33]

Situations like these make us laugh, but at work, tech-challenged people mostly make us frustrated. These are the people who don't check their text messages, who call you on the phone without texting you first (gasp), who click "reply all" to the entire company with their time-off request, or who mumble about how people "used to just pick up the phone" or "used to go to actual meetings" when you ask them to sign up for Slack.

The problem isn't just that they don't enjoy or value technology; it's that their lack of technical skills can end up torpedoing the efficiency and effectiveness of the team. That's why we get frustrated with these people, and that's why they're complicated.

When that happens—and it will—don't assume they are just stubborn or stupid. Remember how fast the world is changing, and keep in mind that you and I could be in their shoes once Generation Alpha hits the workplace. Who knows what tech "those kids" will be adept at or how often they'll roll their eyes at our mistakes and missteps?

How do you handle a complicated person like this? It depends on your role on the team and your relationship with the person, but it mostly comes down to understanding and patience. Try to meet them where they are and understand their mental blocks. Then provide the assistance they need to move forward, such as time, training, or mentoring. Consider building redundancy into your workflow and not relying entirely on one online tool. You might even want to schedule regular meetings—I mean real-life ones—so they don't feel lost in the virtual void.

One more reminder: don't equate people's technological clumsiness with a lack of value or competency. They are more than their tech skills (or lack thereof). Just because they can't back up their data to the cloud doesn't mean they can't offer invaluable insights to your team.

Now let's look at the other extreme. Some people are complicated because *they are so tech-driven that they are unrelatable (or unintelligible) to their team.*

Sometimes these people are the engineers or IT types who forget how much more they know than the average person. But more often than not, these are younger people, those who have grown up with technology and might find it easier to navigate the workplace virtually than to have face-to-face interactions.

If you have a complicated person like this in your office, don't immediately assume they are arrogant, immature, or incapable of living in the real world, any more than you want them to assume you are stubborn, stuck in your ways, or living in a past decade.

INSTEAD, WORK ON BUILDING A BRIDGE.

How can you connect with them? Could you use technology to collaborate with them more effectively? Remember, the older you become, the more likely it will be that a large portion of your coworkers fall into this tech-savvy category, so you need to figure out best practices for bridging the technology gap before you get left behind.

On a practical level, if you want to relate better to these people, try taking a class or watching YouTube videos to get up to speed. Or, reach out and ask them for help. They might laugh at you a little (hopefully in a good-natured way), but I think you'll be surprised by how willing people are to help you when you show interest in their world. Don't underestimate the value of practice, either. These tech-savvy people know what they know because they learned it over time. There's no shame in being further behind them if you're in a different season of life or were born in a different decade. Just keep learning, keep trying, and keep practicing. Things will start to click and the intimidation factor will go way down.

Regardless of where you land on the TQ spectrum, I'd encourage you to lean into the potential that technology has for human connection. It's your ally in breaking down barriers between you and your complicated colleagues. We can get so focused on efficiency, learning curves, and adoption rates that we forget that technology is mostly about finding better ways to communicate and collaborate with living, breathing humans.

- **Share a funny meme in the team chat.**
- **Text people to celebrate their birthdays.**
- **Praise their accomplishments, or just say hi.**
- **Post something thought-provoking that your team can see.**
- **Use social media to get a conversation going.**
- **Share an interesting article or a relevant podcast.**
- **Research professional contacts on LinkedIn.**
- **Use social media to slide (professionally) into someone's DMs.**

These are just a few of the countless ways that tech can improve the quality and depth of your human connections.

Will technology solve all of your people problems? No, of course not. But if you can learn to use it thoughtfully and wisely in a way that builds bridges, you'll be surprised by how many connections can be built, maintained, and improved—even with complicated people.

5. DQ CONNECTION: DECENCY AND KINDNESS

Maybe you've heard the phrase, "It's not personal; it's business."

While that might be a common mantra, it's going to be incredibly difficult to work with complicated people if everything is "just business," at least in today's workplace and with today's generations. As long as you're working with *persons,* things are going to be *personal.*

There's a better way to lead and work than just focusing on business, and it involves connecting to your humanity instead of separating yourself from it. It's called being a decent human being, and it's the foundation of the next People Q we're going to explore: DQ.

Of the five Qs we're exploring, DQ is probably the least well-known. Actually, if you're like me, you might associate those two letters more with a certain ice cream chain than with a people skill. And yet, when it comes to effective collaboration with people with complicated habits, styles, and personalities, this might be the best skill of them all.

The acronym stands for *decency quotient*, and it was highlighted in a 2019 *Harvard Business Review* article by Bill Boulding, dean of Duke University's Fuqua School of Business. Boulding states that DQ means someone "has not only empathy for employees and colleagues but also the genuine desire to care for them" and that it "implies a focus on doing right by others."[34]

While DQ isn't a scientific measurement tool, and it's not something that has been studied as much as IQ or EQ, I think it brings an important human quality into the conversation.

After all, you can be a really smart person—and also a really bad one. You can also be great at understanding emotions yet use that skill to gaslight, guilt-trip, manipulate, blame-shift, or otherwise emotionally abuse people. Boulding continues, "Intellect and emotional intelligence are important, but it's decency that ensures IQ and EQ are used to benefit society, not tear it down."

We're not just talking about being a decent person, but about using this skill to establish connections. For me, the idea of DQ connection describes the ability to connect with people on a human level. For example:

- **ARE YOU kind?**

- **DO YOU consider the impact your actions have on others?**

- **DO YOU have empathy for what other people are experiencing?**

- **DO YOU act in ways that are considered good and moral?**

- **CAN PEOPLE trust your motives?**

- **DO YOU keep other people's best interests in mind in addition to your own?**

- **DO YOU act with integrity rather than sacrificing anything for growth or profit?**

- **DO PEOPLE feel safe around you?**

Being nice and getting your work done should not be mutually exclusive goals. There's no reason you shouldn't be able to be kind *and* effective. Polite *and* productive. Compassionate *and* competitive. Understanding *and* demanding.

Too often we leave the human component on the side, as if it were optional, when in reality it's an essential key to a happy, effective workplace. As the *Harvard Business Review* states,

> **NUMEROUS STUDIES SHOW THAT** when leaders are primarily focused on the well-being of their employees, this is a strong predictor of employee job satisfaction, perceived organizational support, loyalty and trust in the organization, and retention. It also has been linked with improved employee job performance (by boosting employee motivation), and better team performance.[35]

But what about the whole "nice guys finish last" thing? Sure, it sounds wonderful to be a nice boss, a generous leader, a kind coworker, or a caring employee, but won't you get trampled and left in the dust by all the hard-driving types who know how to "get ahead"?

Researchers from the University of California, Berkeley, conducted two fourteen-year studies to attempt to find out if nice guys really do finish last. They evaluated how much power several hundred participants gained over the course of time and looked for correlations to how selfish, combative, or manipulative they were. They summarized their findings this way:

> **SELFISH, DECEITFUL, AND AGGRESSIVE** individuals were no more likely to attain power than were generous, trustworthy, and nice individuals. Why not? Disagreeable individuals were intimidating, which would have elevated their power, but they also had poorer interpersonal relationships at work, which offset any possible power advantage their behavior might have provided.[36]

In other words, the bullies didn't get any further ahead than the non-bullies. They just had more bodies under their bus.

While there is much research that backs up the value of kindness in the workplace, you probably understand this intuitively, just by being a real human being with feelings and needs of your own. Think about your own employment experiences. What kind of boss do you respond best to: someone who bullies and intimidates you, or someone who respects and empowers you? What kind of work environment brings out the best in you and those you work with: a toxic, cutthroat, dog-eat-dog culture, or one where teamwork is encouraged and people are allowed to thrive?

If you're going to build a successful career, you need to focus on more than your knowledge base, emotional intelligence, change management skills, and tech prowess.

YOU ALSO NEED TO BE A DECENT HUMAN BEING.

Of course, if you're going to work with complicated people, your decency is going to be put to the test. After all, anybody can be nice to nice people and polite to polite people. It's not hard to be generous and caring to colleagues you like and who like you back. But can you treat difficult, frustrating, irritating, and confusing people with courtesy and concern?

That's where DQ really comes into play.

Can you be a *decent* person when you're dealing with a *complicated* person?

I'm talking about the manager who takes the credit for things you did. The coworker who is constantly negative. The board member who always interrupts your presentation with condescending questions. The colleague who makes fun of you behind your back. The client who asks for eight different quotes and then buys from the competition. The boss who refuses to even consider the remote possibility that maybe, possibly, perchance, they could be wrong about something.

I'm not saying you have to like them, but can you be nice to them? Can you consider their needs as well as your own?

This is more of a skill and a decision than a personality trait. It's a learned behavior. It's an internal choice any of us can make to look beyond efficiency and effectiveness, beyond timelines and bottom lines, beyond our egos and emotions, until we can see others on a human level.

The heart of the DQ connection is this: treat people like you would want to be treated. This is also known as the Golden Rule, and it's a timeless and time-tested way to evaluate your actions. Don't get tunnel vision, thinking only of the project at hand, company profits, or your own interests. Those things matter, but they're not *all* that matters. Try to balance everyone's interests and make decisions that take all parties into account.

The stress and pressure of business might try to squeeze the humanity out of us, but we can reclaim it. Inside most of us—if not all of us—there's a good person with a good heart. There's a decent, caring, fair, altruistic, compassionate, empathetic soul who knows instinctively how to treat others. That's the side of you that needs to bubble up when you're dealing with people, especially the not-so-nice ones.

CUE THE Q REVIEW

When people get complicated, you don't have to match their negative energy. You don't have to fight dirty just because they do. You'll only make a complicated situation more complicated. Instead, use your People Qs to manage your thoughts, emotions, and interactions and to respond with maturity. To review:

1. **Your IQ Connection** (intelligence quotient) describes how well you connect with others on an intellectual or knowledge level. What do you need to learn and know in order to work better with someone else?

2. **Your EQ Connection** (emotional intelligence quotient) refers to how you handle the emotional side of relationships and teamwork. What are you feeling, what are they feeling, and how can you navigate that minefield wisely?

3. **Your AQ Connection** (adaptability quotient) is about how quickly and effectively you adjust to people's differences. Can you pivot and change where needed in order to work with a wide range of people?

4. **Your TQ Connection** (technology quotient) examines your ability to interact with people using technology. Can you leverage technology to build bridges with others, even if their proficiency or preferences are different from yours?

5. **Your DQ Connection** (decency quotient) describes the "human" side of your connections: your kindness, generosity, and care for others. Do you consider the needs and feelings of the people who work with you?

You're going to need all five of these People Qs to deal with the particular class of complicated people we're going to look at next. I'm talking about the infamous generation gap.

If you've ever rolled your eyes at your older boss who seems so old-school or told someone that the younger generation is rotting their brains with their cell phone addiction, this next chapter is for you.

CHAPTER 7

AGE IS JUST A NUMBER... UNTIL YOU HAVE TO WORK TOGETHER

I was on an airplane, pondering strategies to take my company to the next level, when the idea struck me: I should hire my mom as a research assistant. My mom was born in 1949 and gave birth to me in 1986. She joined the American workforce in the late 1960s, and I started receiving W-2 income in the early 2000s. So there are almost four decades of age and working experience between her and me.

I suspected I was in for a wild ride, but nothing could have prepared me for having to explain to her how we leverage artificial intelligence for maximizing, curating, and scheduling content. We even utilize AI to create content in different languages, using my computer-generated avatar and voice to influence people around the world in their own language. I wish you could have seen my dear mom's face when I began to elucidate the inner workings of the rapidly evolving, wildly exhilarating AI universe. It was like trying to teach a goldfish to ride a bicycle.

Nevertheless, it's fun having Mom as a part of the squad. More than fun, it's eye-opening, refreshing, and helpful. She adds things nobody else could add. The more diversity in age and work experience you can have on a team, the better.

Right?

(Cue weak applause.)

Let's be honest. On paper it sounds great to mesh multiple decades in the workplace, but in real life, it can be a real pain in the I'm-not-going-to-finish-that-sentence. Now, Mom is amazing, and it's working well for us. But in general, age differences seem to be a flash point for people in every area of life, and work is no exception.

So let's dive headfirst into the often turbulent waters of navigating generational differences in the workplace to lay out some invaluable insights on how to work with the complicated folks born decades apart from us. It's time to bridge the generation gap and make the workplace a harmonious space for everyone, from Baby Boomers to Gen Z.

GENERATIONS, AGES, AND SEASONS OF LIFE

As you've probably noticed, when people talk about other generations, it's often based on stereotypes, and it usually focuses on negative traits. People tend to have certain beliefs about Gen Z, Millennials, Gen X, or Boomers—beliefs that are based on a mix of experiences they've had and clickbait headlines they've read.

That's a problem for three reasons.

FIRST, you can't lump literally billions of people under one label and expect it to be completely accurate. To dismiss entire age ranges of people by saying things like "they are so entitled" or "they are so stuck in their ways" is simplistic and, quite frankly, mean. We need to scale back the rhetoric and scale up the empathy. You can't spend ten minutes Googling "Gen Z" and expect to predict the behavior of every twenty-five-year-old out there.

SECOND, generations are a construct. That means we made them up. They are loosely defined labels that attempt to simplify things for the sake of discussion, but at the end of the day, they are just words, not biological definitions of distinct species. There is no consensus on how to determine exactly when a generation starts or ends, and there's no official body that names them or describes them. You'll find a variety of date ranges for most generations, and the lines between them are a bit fuzzy. If you're on the border between generations (sometimes called *cuspers*), don't feel obligated to pick a side. You're probably a mix anyway.

THIRD, and maybe most importantly, many of the "differences" between generations are at least partly connected to the current ages and seasons of life of the people within them. As generations move along the timeline of life, the people that make them up change a little. Or a lot. The rebellious, change-focused hippies of the 1970s are today's senior citizens, so don't assume that just because the Boomers you know act a certain way today means they've always been that way.

The same goes for Gen Z. Before you critique the amount of time they spend on social media, consider the fact that many of them don't have kids or mortgages yet, so time is a luxury they can enjoy. They have no idea what's coming. (Cue evil laughter.) Writer Roger Allen is quoted as saying, "In case you're worried about what's going to become of the younger generation, it's going to grow up and start worrying about the younger generation."[37]

You might be one of the youngest members of your team right now, and you're chomping at the bit to take risks and innovate. But thirty years from now, you could be the oldest team member who is pulling back on the reins, trying to slow things down to a safer speed. Both are valid, and both are needed. Stay humble.

The different seasons of life affect how people show up at work. More specifically, they can make people more complicated at work. Consider for a moment the potential impact of these seasons:

- **A college student who is also working part-time or full-time**

- **A single adult who is focused on their career (but has regular dating drama)**

- **Someone who just got married**

- **The parent of small kids who don't sleep through the night and demand constant attention (especially if they're a single parent)**

- **A parent with older kids who need less supervision but have real emergencies and constant teenage angst**

- **Someone going through a messy divorce**

- **Someone who has recently become an empty nester with time on their hands and money in the bank**

- **Someone dealing with illness, death in the family, or another tragedy**

- **An older adult staring down retirement, maybe with no idea what to do next or how to pay for it**

Each of these seasons will tend to affect how people feel, how they act, and how you experience them. Since some are loosely connected to age, we might be tempted to lump their complications under a generational label, but that's often unfair and unhelpful. It's better to take a step back and ask whether someone's complication could be related to a season they are going through. That means treating them as the individuals they are rather than as part of a faceless category.

Anita Lettink, an author and speaker who specializes in HR and the future of work, argues for this point when she writes, "The differences within a generation can be far larger than the differences between them. While there are similar characteristics within a generation because of shared experiences . . . everyone is different. Everyone's circumstances are different. One size never fits all."[38]

Bottom line: I'm convinced that "generations" are more complicated than we've sometimes made them out be, and we probably aren't as far apart as we might think. If we can learn to walk a mile in the flip-flops, Crocs, New Balances, or Oxford wingtips of other age groups, we can probably understand them more quickly than we originally assumed.

And as I've said over and over, understanding is key to collaboration.

This matters because you will *always* work with people from other generations. You won't be able to avoid them all, ignore them all, or cancel them all. They're going to be working at the desk next to you. They're going to be on your project team. They're going to be sitting on your board. They're going to be setting your company policies. They're going to be leading you and training you, and you're going to be leading them and training them. They're going to be your partners, your shareholders, your customers, your clients, your contractors, your employees.

Instead of letting those differences intimidate us, we need to let them intrigue us. Instead of moving away from people who are decades apart, we need to move closer.

That's easier than you might think.

ONE MINOR ADJUSTMENT AWAY

Age-based conflict is both anti-productive and avoidable, and it makes things more complicated than they need to be. No, it's not always easy to get along with people who were born decades before or after you, but it's also not as hard as you might assume.

Thanks to my sneaker addiction, my go-to outfit when I speak at events and conferences is a suit and Nikes. Classy meets comfortable—that's my happy place.

One of my clients is a commercial real estate company based in Tampa, and the CEO is an older woman who admires my shoes every time I speak for them. One time she told me, "Ryan, I could never pull that off. I couldn't wear shoes like that."

So I sent her a pair.

I talked to her later, and I asked her if she wore them. She said not only did she wear them, but the entire office noticed, and they loved them, especially the younger employees.

It's amazing how something as small as a wardrobe adjustment can build a connection with people born three decades after you. It was a small act, almost a symbolic one, but it built a bridge, and her office was better because of it.

I wonder, how often are we one minor adjustment away from building bridges to other generations? We can get so intimidated by the gulf between age groups, the dreaded generation gap. But are people from other age groups, seasons of life, and generations really that different from us?

The answer is both yes and no.

Yes, there are differences between people in different decades or stages of life. And yes, those differences can absolutely make people complicated. A twenty-year-old doesn't merely dress differently than a sixty-year-old. Often, they see the world differently. They approach work differently. They have a different relationship with technology. They have different boundaries, different expectations, and different communication styles. Trying to work on a project or staff a department with a multigenerational team means merging those differences—and often, some gear-grinding happens as a result.

But the answer is also no, they are not that different. We are actually more similar to each other than we are dissimilar. Generational research consistently finds more commonalities than differences among generations.[39] Our survey showed the same thing. While there were some interesting age-based nuances in certain topics, in general, age and generational differences weren't a hugely differentiating factor.

That's a good thing.

It's important to recognize the ties that bind us, not just the quirks that frustrate us. After all, we are all first and foremost humans, not Boomers or Gen X or Millennials or Gen Z. We're from different generations, not different planets. You might never understand why your co-worker won't answer their phone but posts memes on your work Slack channel at two in the morning, but you can take one step closer to them. You can learn skills to communicate with them, receive from them, and succeed alongside them.

We are closer to each other than we often think, and small, empathetic acts—like a CEO wearing sneakers to the office—can accomplish more than we often realize.

As I said above, we can't be simplistic or naive when it comes to generational labels and stereotypes. But that doesn't mean the concept of generations isn't a helpful tool for understanding people.

We just have to use it right.

We need to identify points of connection as well as points of conflict. As we take a closer look at the generations currently represented in the workplace, I'm going to avoid the "OK Boomer" and "TikTok kids" stereotypes. Instead, I want to focus on how to understand each other and collaborate better.

GENERATIONS IN THE WORKPLACE

There are five main generations currently influencing the workplace, although the oldest one is much less represented due to their age. According to the Pew Research Center, a respected think tank and polling firm, the generations in the workplace are:

- **The Silent Generation: born 1928–1945**
- **Baby Boomers: born 1946–1964**
- **Generation X: born 1965–1980**
- **Millennials: born 1981–1996**
- **Generation Z: born 1997–2012**[40, 41]

Eventually, we're going to have another generation joining the workforce: Generation Alpha. Today, the oldest members of this group are focused on surviving middle school, and the youngest ones haven't been born yet. But around 2030, they'll be collecting their first paychecks.

The term "generation" can be defined as "a group of people born around the same time and raised around the same place."[42] It's basically a bunch of people who popped into the world around the same time and grew up in similar settings. Think of it as a club you didn't choose but got a lifetime membership to. Generations are these broad categories we slap on people based on their birth year and shared global mixtapes.

On a general level, people who were born and raised in similar circumstances tend to share similar values and ways of thinking. Why should we care about this, especially at work? Here's why: Age gaps in the office aren't just about who remembers dial-up Internet and who was born swiping a screen. It's about understanding the mindset that comes with your coworker's vintage. It's about realizing that your sixty-year-old boss might not get your meme references, but they have wisdom worth listening to.

If you are going to work effectively with people who are multiple decades younger or older than you, you need to understand how they think, what they fear, what they value, how they communicate, how they approach technology, and more.

Just as importantly, you need to understand *yourself.* Like everyone else, you were born into a specific generation. You are a specific age. You are experiencing a unique season of life. You are a generation-specific cocktail of experiences and quirks, and that makes you complicated to somebody.

In our survey, one of the more fascinating findings related to generations came from the question, "Which generation do you consider the most complicated to deal with at work?"

Can you guess? Go ahead and try.

Naturally, it depended on who we asked. We found that Millennials consider Gen X and Boomers the most complicated generations to work with, while Gen X and Boomers both consider Millennials the most complicated. Meanwhile (and I find this hilarious), Gen Z considers their own generation to be the most complicated. At least they're honest.

That makes sense, if you think about it. At the time of our survey (2024), Millennials, Gen X, and Boomers make up three-quarters of the workforce, and they have most of the higher-paying job roles. They are currently engaged in a lot of pushing and pulling over who gets which job in what company. So the finger-pointing is normal.

If we repeat the survey in ten years, will we get the same results? Probably not. The majority of Boomers will have aged out of the workforce. A good chunk of Gen X will be eyeing retirement. Gen Z will be a much larger group, nipping at the heels of Millennials and competing for control. And a new generation, Gen Alpha, is going to be on the scene. If I had to guess who would be doing the most finger-pointing at each other in ten years, I'd say the two biggest groups: Millennials and Gen Z.

What this data tells me is not that one generation is inherently better or worse than another, but that they are complicated *to each other.*

And that, my friend, means no generation is a lost cause. Rather than letting generational differences devolve into generational warfare, we can learn to collaborate together more effectively through empathy and knowledge.

The fact that the workforce will always have large segments from multiple generations means we'll continually be building bridges across the generation gap. For however many years you have left in the workforce, you're going to be surrounded by people who are multiple decades older or younger than you. That is not going away.

AND THAT'S A GOOD THING.
DIVERSITY ALWAYS IS.

HOW TO WORK WELL WITH OTHER GENERATIONS

What are some best practices for working with people from other generations, especially when the age and worldview differences are complicated? Let me give you three:

I. THINK ABOUT HOW YOU THINK ABOUT AGE

Pay attention to how you look at people younger and older than you. Do you have any age-related prejudices?

Mark Twain is believed to have said, "When I was a boy of fourteen, my father was so ignorant I could hardly stand to have the old man around. But when I got to be twenty-one, I was astonished at how much the old man had learned in seven years."[43] In other words, the older you get, the more you appreciate the wisdom that people older than you have had all along.

Research has found that in general, we tend to rate older people as warmer and friendlier than younger people but also as less competent, less ambitious, less responsible, and less mentally proficient. In addition, we are more likely to attribute memory failures of older adults to intellectual incompetence, but we view memory failures of younger adults as simply a lack of attention or effort.[44]

That's scary. It means we often let someone's age skew our perception of their capabilities and qualities, even without knowing them. This is called *ageism,* and it refers to evaluative judgments about people based simply on their advanced age. Ageism probably doesn't get as much airtime as racism, misogyny, or other areas of social prejudice, but it's just as real.

Age-based prejudice can also flow in the other direction: toward those much younger than us. As a speaker and coach, I've been in many meetings where people from different generations were in the same room or on the same Zoom, and it's fascinating (and concerning) to watch the body language of some older people when younger team members take the floor.

Usually it's not animosity as much as it is disinterest. Dismissal. Disconnection. There's a sense that the younger person doesn't have a lot to bring to the table. The body language and reactions of some older people seem to say, "There's no way this kid can add perspective. They don't have my education or experience. I'll let them talk because it's not worth arguing with them, but I'm not going to learn anything."

All age-based prejudice is wrong. Why? Because it ignores the actual capabilities of the person. "He's too old to work on a technology product" or "She's too young to lead a team" are not logical statements. They are stereotype-based value judgments that reduce human beings to a cliché, to an assumption, to a dismissive trope.

The funny thing is that "young" and "old" are relative. We all know this. The older you get, the further out you slide the "old" marker in your mental definition. "Old" is always at least a couple of decades past where you currently are in life, and "young and immature" is always a decade or so behind you.

Here's something that works with every generation: just give people the thing they want the most—to feel important. If you're going to work with people from other generations, you have to start by respecting them. You have to acknowledge and then intentionally subvert the subconscious biases that creep in.

To their credit, I've watched CEOs who are much older and more successful than I am do exactly that when they bring me in to speak to their companies. Executives from Fortune 100 corporations worth billions of dollars have pulled me aside and said, "Hey, I'd love to pick your brain for a few minutes." And I'm thinking, *What are you talking about? Pick my brain? I need to pick your brain. I want to hear you talk.* It's both surprising and challenging to me because I hope I always stay open to people who are younger than I am.

Only you can control your perspective and your mental conversation. When you consider that difficult, complicated person from another generation, whether they are younger or older than you, what words run through your mind? If they are negative and dismissive, try reframing them.

When it comes to people younger than you:

ARE THEY

- **DISRESPECTFUL . . .**
  or are they passionate and enthusiastic?

- **LAZY . . .**
  or do they care about work-life balance?

- **ADDICTED TO SCREENS . . .**
  or are they skilled at using digital tools?

When it comes to people older than you:

ARE THEY

- **OVER THE HILL . . .**
  or do they have a lot of experience?

- **SET IN THEIR WAYS . . .**
  or do they know something you don't?

- **OUT OF TOUCH . . .**
  or do they just touch a different part of the world than you?

My guess is that the answer to some of these questions will be "a little bit of both." That's okay. Give people space to be human.

Instead of focusing on how they make your life more complicated, appreciate their unique experiences and perspectives without judgment or bias. Work is complicated enough without superimposing age-based assumptions on people.

2. BE INTENTIONAL ABOUT WORKING TOGETHER

It's hard to build cross-generational teams, but it's worth it. Everyone brings something to the table that everyone else needs.

To be honest, I see more generations throwing a bone than building a bridge. They're willing to show some consideration or grant some concessions to other generations, but that's as far as they go. It's not anger or angst; it's avoidance. They don't think ill of each other because they don't think much about each other at all.

They simply nod their heads at each other, dance around delicate topics, and then go off and do their own thing. But is that really all we can hope for? Tolerance in public, dismissiveness in private, and ongoing disconnection in the workplace? I would argue strongly that if that's what we're settling for, we're missing out on the strength and beauty found in diversity.

The goal isn't to ignore their age, any more than you ignore someone's ethnicity or gender. Those things matter to that person. They are part of who they are and the life they've lived. Just make sure you see the value in those things rather than using them as labels to diminish or dismiss them.

How can you be intentional about working cross-generationally? On a personal level, you can take proactive steps to connect relationally with people from other generations, to ask questions about their life stories, and to receive from their strengths, talents, training, and experience. On a more general level, companies can ensure that apprenticeships and training programs are open to workers of all ages, create cross-generational mentoring programs to help facilitate knowledge transfer, and actively recruit talent from all ages.

At the end of the day, this is about attitude and intentionality.

IF YOU TRULY VALUE A MULTI-GENERATIONAL TEAM, YOU NEED TO PUT IN THE WORK TO BUILD ONE.

3. ERR ON THE SIDE OF INNOVATION

When in doubt, err on the side of innovation. Usually, this means moving younger rather than older.

Now, I've said a lot about respecting the experience and wisdom of older generations, so don't take this the wrong way. I'm not saying to hire only young people or to give control of the company to Gen Z. All I'm saying is that in this tricky business of building multigenerational companies, innovation and constant reinvention are key, so pay attention to what is new, what is fresh, and what is changing.

It's often human nature to do the opposite, especially when you've worked really hard to get where you are today, and you know there is a lot at stake. While people of all ages should take the initiative to build bridges, I think older generations have a greater responsibility in this area because history only flows in one direction, at least until somebody invents a time machine. People are always going to get older, and new generations are always going to be born. So in order to build a sustainable company or business, you have to continually make room for younger people and new generations.

It's a cycle as old as humanity. Over time, more and more coworkers and customers are going to be younger than you simply because time marches on. The question is, will you march with it? Unless you are intentional about opening yourself up to a young, fresh, new, and scarily unfamiliar future, inertia will take over . . . and you will be passed over.

I was speaking at a conference in the health industry a while back, and as part of my prep for the talk, I met with a number of executives and leaders in the field. The conversation turned to technology. They shared that they were implementing online tools to improve staff communication and patient care. However, there was resistance among some of the older employees who didn't want to change their preferred working style just to meet the preferences of their younger coworkers.

As we talked further, the big idea that emerged was that the demographic of their patients was changing, not just their staff. This wasn't about catering to the whims of coworkers who wanted screens and apps and text messages. It was about serving a younger customer base that expected and needed cutting-edge technology.

A few days later when I spoke at the conference, that was the perspective I took. I didn't try to convince anyone to adopt an app or switch to a new software program. Rather, I spoke about doing whatever was necessary to meet the evolving needs of their customers. That included using tools their customers would understand the best . . . and that meant change. In order to serve others well, sometimes we have to lay down what's comfortable for us and consider what's best for them.

Younger generations have to do their part too. As I said above, older people bring a great deal to the table, and young people would be wise to listen more than they talk and to learn with humility. But eventually, the younger people will become the older people, and the cycle of change and adaptation will repeat, so learn to err on the side of innovation, change, and reinvention.

We all need essentially the same things, regardless of the year we were born. In the 1940s, psychologist Abraham Maslow famously outlined many of these in what is called "Maslow's hierarchy of needs."[45] These needs are often represented in a pyramid, and they include physiological needs such as food, water, and shelter, as well as safety needs, social needs, self-esteem needs, and self-actualization needs.

While Maslow's model doesn't include every human need, it illustrates an important point: whether we are eighteen or eighty-five, at our core, we all need, want, and pursue similar things. We are concerned about both surviving and thriving, about avoiding death and enjoying life. We think about money a lot, and about food, friends, love, getting more sleep, and doing things we enjoy. We strive to minimize pain and maximize pleasure. We long to live a satisfied life and do meaningful work.

While each generation puts its own spin on these things, at our core, the same internal drivers have been motivating humans for thousands of years. Hidden behind other people's weird comments and behaviors are the same basic hopes, fears, and dreams that drive our own weird comments and behaviors.

The problem is that it's all too easy to let age differences make people seem less human. It can be hard to imagine that someone who is a few decades younger or older than you struggles with the same things you do. We tend to see them as "others," as different than us. But they want to fit in and be liked, as you probably do. They want to have a fulfilling romantic life, as you probably do. They are scared of running out of money, just as you might be.

It takes intentionality and human decency to look past the flip-flops, lattes, selfies, wrinkles, dress pants, sneakers, emojis, slang, or whatever other superficial marker triggers that in-group/out-group response. But if you can connect to complicated people on the level of their needs, you'll have a lot more patience for the way they express those needs, and you'll be able to work more effectively and graciously together.

People of all ages—even the complicated ones—have a lot to offer. So let's build bridges instead of burning them; let's listen to each other instead of laughing at each other; and let's dialogue with other generations instead of dismissing them.

We're in the same boat and on the same bus. Even though we might argue about where we're going, how to get there, and who gets to drive, ultimately, we are all in this together. Whether we're old-timers, upstarts, or somewhere in between, we need to learn from one another, lean on each other, and build better workplaces together.

Our collaboration with other generations will rise or fall depending on how well we're able to communicate with people who are different than us. That's the case with *all* bridge-building, though, isn't it?

> **If we're going to understand complicated people well enough to work together, grow together, and succeed together, we have to become WORLD-CLASS COMMUNICATORS.**

That's the topic we're going to explore next.

CHAPTER 8

NOW YOU'RE SPEAKING MY LANGUAGE

I always enjoy hearing people read other people's text messages out loud. It's a riot, particularly when a woman channels her inner dude, giving voice to his texts in the tone she's convinced he used, or when a guy does his best impression of a woman, laying it on how he figures she typed those words. You can almost hear the voice of the sender in your head protesting, *Wait, that's not how I said that!*

I think if any of us heard our own text messages, emails, or other written communication read aloud, we'd often say the same thing: "That's not how I said that! That's not what I meant! You're reading into it! You're missing the point!"

Written communication isn't all that tends to get misinterpreted. You can have a verbal conversation among five people, and when you walk away, there will be five different ideas of what was said and what was meant by it.

The reality is that there is often a gap between what's coming out of our mouths and what's going into their ears. We might assume we are great communicators and that everyone around us knows exactly what we mean, but that's probably not true. Communication is always at least slightly broken because we are imperfect, complicated humans trying to get our points across to other imperfect, complicated humans.

> **This includes communication at work. In our survey, "communication style" was identified by 43% of respondents as one of the top three factors that make people difficult to work with, and "communication and conflict management training" was the top-ranked suggestion for companies to reduce the negative impact of complicated people at work. Similarly, in a 2021 poll by Gallup, only 7% of respondents strongly agreed that communication at their place of work was "accurate, timely and open." That means the other 93% felt there was clear room for improvement in one or all of these areas.[46]**

Communication isn't a new problem. In 1950, a journalist and business writer named William Whyte published an article called "Is Anybody Listening?" that promoted better business communication. He wrote, "The great enemy of communication, we find, is the illusion of it."[47] Both the article title and that quote are as relevant today as they were back then. Communication is one of those issues where, the moment you believe you're good at it, you're probably not.

Nowhere is this communication gap more evident—and potentially more dangerous—than when you're working with complicated people. It's challenging enough to avoid misunderstandings when the person on the other end of the call, email, direct message, conference table, or in-person convo is someone you see eye to eye with. It's a whole new level of crazy when you're dealing with someone who is challenging or difficult.

Unfortunately, it's all too easy to give up on communicating rather than getting better at it.

> **In our study, we found that while 78% of workers deal with complicated people at least weekly, only 41% say they "often" or "constantly" engage in open communication with complicated individuals. That is, 8 out of 10 of us *deal* with complicated people regularly, but only 4 out of 10 of us are regularly *communicating* with complicated people. That's a little bit of a red flag to me, and it's something we want to explore with further research.**

Open communication should be key to any interaction with complicated people, and yet less than half of us engage in it regularly. Are these people simply avoiding their complicated peers? Refusing to engage with them? Keeping their communication as short as possible?

If you're dealing with complicated individuals regularly, take a fresh look at your communication style and skills. Specifically, consider two important factors: the *direction* and the *medium*.

First, the direction. Within the structure of your organization, are you talking to people above you, below you, or on your level? Each direction requires a different strategy if you want to be effective.

Second, the medium. Are you writing emails, making phone calls, navigating virtual or hybrid work environments, or doing that old-fashioned thing where you talk to people in person? Every form of communication requires a unique approach.

In the pages ahead, we're going to look at practical strategies for communicating with people—especially the complicated ones—while considering both of these factors.

DIRECTION: DO YOU KNOW WHO YOU'RE TALKING TO?

In communication, who you're talking to changes everything. Just think about how you'd say something as simple as "no" to a few different people. For example: your parents, your spouse, your kids or other children, that one neighbor you like, that other neighbor you don't like, a police officer who just pulled you over . . . you get the picture. You'd change everything from your tone to your posture to your wording, depending on the person on the other end of your "no."

When it comes to the "who" in the workplace, it's helpful to think directionally.

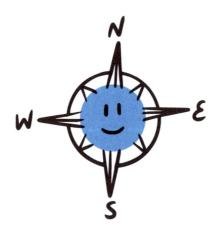

YOU HAVE TO CONSIDER WHETHER YOU'RE SPEAKING

UP

ACROSS

DOWN OR

That is, within the particular structure and hierarchy of your company, are you communicating to people who LEAD YOU, people YOU LEAD, or people who are on the SAME LEVEL as you? To put it another way, are you dealing with a COMPLICATED BOSS, a COMPLICATED DIRECT REPORT, or a COMPLICATED COWORKER?

SPEAKING UP
Vibing with Unicorns

Let's start with how you talk to your boss, directors, or C-suite executives. Even if they aren't complicated personalities, the mere fact they have so much power over your workday, job role, and career trajectory is complicated. And if, on top of that, they *are* complicated . . . then you've got your work cut out for you.

Working for a complicated person is like trying to do your job with one arm tied behind your back. It handicaps your productivity, messes with your mind, and tanks your morale.

Unsurprisingly, that has a direct impact on employee retention. In our recent research, we found that 44% of working Americans have quit a job because their boss was too complicated to work with, including 50% of Gen Z, the highest of any generation. That blew me away. At one point or another, nearly half the workforce has chosen the nuclear option of quitting because their boss was impossibly complicated, they didn't know how to handle their complicated boss, or both.

Assuming you don't want to quit every time you have to deal with a complicated leader, you need to be able to communicate upward. The problem is that approaching the bigwigs at work can feel like trying to have a heart-to-heart with a unicorn. You know they are out there, you know they are rare, you know having better interactions with them could change everything . . . but actually meeting with them in real life? Truly getting their attention and having their ear? Good luck.

It's helpful to acknowledge the elephant in the boardroom here: this can be scary. You're not alone in feeling like you're about to walk the plank when you hit "send" on that email or step into their office. You're not the only one who freezes up making awkward small talk when you step into the elevator and find yourself face-to-face with a unicorn in an Armani suit.

Staying silent is not a good long-term option, though. You have to send your ideas, feedback, and sometimes SOS signals up the chain of command to your managers, directors, and even those elusive C-suite execs. You have to speak up, and that means speaking *up*—upward in the org chart.

I know that sounds scary to some, but it doesn't have to be. Your leaders are people just like you, and you know how to talk to people. You do it every day. So, let's look at some ways to speak up and speak *up*.

1. LEARN TO SPEAK C-SUITE.

When communicating with your leadership, share what you have to say in their language. In my coaching practice, this is one of the things we often emphasize with mid- and upper-level managers in particular.

Communicating effectively with C-suite executives—such as CEOs, CFOs, COOs, and CIOs—and other high-level leadership requires that you frame your information or request in the context of what your leadership is aiming for and cares about, and you have to do it using terms and concepts that make sense to them. Your communication with them needs to fit within their strategic, high-level perspective.

One way to do this is by understanding and utilizing key business concepts that resonate with them. This goes beyond just memorizing technical terms such as ROI, KPI, scalability, stakeholder engagement, sustainability, risk management, and value proposition. It's also about understanding why that language matters and framing your conversation to align with their goals. It's about learning what matters to the people upstream, then finding strategies to get your message across.

Keep in mind that your competency is being evaluated more than you might realize. That's not meant to scare you, but rather to prepare you. I spoke with an executive recently who had just come from a meeting with the new owner of the company. The owner told this executive that she was looking for one thing in her leadership team: competency. She didn't need everyone to be good at *her* job; she needed them to be good at *their* jobs and to know *their* stuff.

That's the mindset you should take into conversations with executives, managers, business owners, and anyone else who sits higher on the org chart than you. If you communicate from a place of competency and knowledge, you can't go wrong.

2. STAY READY SO YOU DON'T HAVE TO GET READY.

One of the biggest mistakes you can make when communicating upward is not being prepared. When you think of preparing to communicate well, your thoughts might jump straight to PowerPoint decks and spreadsheets, but preparation has to start sooner and go deeper than that. Learn to pay attention to the breadcrumbs your leadership continually leaves behind that show you what they value the most. Then, when you're having a conversation or making a presentation, you'll naturally address the concerns and goals they care about the most.

I often use 3 Cs—which stand for *celebrate, champion,* and *complain*—to help teams understand their leaders better.

What do they celebrate?

What do your leaders praise when they see it? Is it punctuality? Presentation? Creativity? Social media presence? Innovation? Problem-solving? Initiative? Hard work? Empathy? Your leadership might not even realize how valuable these things are to them, but when they see them, they celebrate them.

Those are clues. If you can figure out what they want to see more of, you can tailor your conversation to fit those things. This is a conscious decision to get on the same page with them, aligning your time, resources, ideas, and focus with theirs.

What do they champion?

What do they push and promote? Where do they put their money? What line item on the budget do they pay the most attention to? What metrics do they always ask about?

For example, when Mark Cuban bought the Dallas Mavericks in 2000, he decided to focus on fan experience. He attended every game and often sat with fans. He yelled at the refs, which people love, but he also made frequent trips to the soundboard to make sure they were hyping up the crowd enough. He put his email address on the big screen and personally checked his inbox to see what ideas came through. Once a fan complained about not being able to see the shot clock and suggested three-sided clocks. A few weeks later, the court was equipped with brand-new, three-sided shot clocks. The result of all this? Within three years, team revenues more than doubled, merch sales went through the roof, attendance shot up, and an ESPN poll ranked the Mavericks as the number-one team in fan relations.[48]

Is that the only way to run a team? Of course not. Some owners' approach to creating a winning culture is by focusing on building a strong, data-driven front office. Alternatively, there's the strategy of investing heavily in star players, believing that financial investment in top talent is the key to winning championships. When looking at these diverse approaches, we're not talking about "right" or "wrong." Their approaches are *their* approaches. My point is that leaders have values and priorities, and if we are going to uncomplicate our conversations with them, we must understand what those values and priorities are and in what order they are ranked.

What do they complain about?

What bothers them? What irks them? What annoys them? What makes them mad? What makes them disappointed? What do they correct or punish?

Just as with the previous two points, their complaints are breadcrumbs pointing you toward better communication. If you can show them how your idea or request is connected to their pain points, you'll have their ear.

The 3 Cs aren't necessarily posted on a wall somewhere, but if you read through the company-wide emails your leaders send, you can pick them out. They are there for anyone willing to look for them. The question is, are you paying attention?

Discovering these three things is the first half of your homework. The second half is being ready to talk about them. Don't just share your problems, challenges, or needs; bring two or three potential solutions and tie them into the 3 Cs. Leaders appreciate that.

No matter how complicated your leaders might be, tailoring your message to align with what they celebrate, champion, and complain about can turn your words from white noise into music to their ears.

3. VALUE THEIR TIME.

For better or worse, high-level professionals tend to operate under constant stress and on tight schedules. That means your communication with managers, directors, and C-suite executives needs to be both substantial and succinct—i.e., short, sweet, and to the point. That might require some strategy and work on your end.

For instance, if you're presenting a project proposal to an executive, create a bullet-point summary that highlights key objectives, outcomes, and resource requirements, but also be prepared to answer questions and dive into details if prompted. That way, you can be efficient with their time without sacrificing accuracy, and you can respond organically to their interests or doubts rather than trying to force-feed them what you think they want or need to hear.

Talking to leadership doesn't have to be a nerve-wracking episode of *Survivor*. With a bit of prep, a clear message, and a willingness to speak up, you can navigate these conversations like a pro. So do your homework and make your mark. After all, if you don't speak up, who will?

SPEAKING ACROSS
Bridging the Horizontal Communication Gap

Next up: How do you communicate with a complicated peer? Neither of you has direct authority to boss the other around, but you're on the same side. You work for the same company. And at the end of the day, your collaboration is going to either make things better or worse for both of you.

When we asked people to rank which role or category of person tended to have the most complicated individuals in their experience, "coworkers" headed the list, with 55% of people listing it as one of their top two.[49] That doesn't necessarily mean coworkers are more complicated than anyone else. More likely, it points to the fact that this is a numbers game. Many people deal with more coworkers on a regular basis than any other job role, so that's where the problem is most obvious.

> **Interestingly, more than half (53%) say they have more complicated coworkers than their boss or leadership believes, including 62% of Gen Z, the highest of any generation. Not only are they dealing with difficult individuals on a regular basis, but they also don't feel like they have the understanding or support of their leadership.**

That's exactly why you have to know how to communicate *across*. Allow me to share a few suggestions.

1. START WITH RESPECT.

In the case of a peer, you're respecting a few things, including their autonomy as a human being, expertise, experience, knowledge, and finally, their lane or area of responsibility.

That means you don't try to control them or do their job for them, and you don't treat them rudely, even if they kind of deserve it. You can make suggestions, especially if their difficult behavior is causing problems for you, but you can't really force them to do anything they don't want to do. You can't swoop in and demand they conform to your ideals.

While you might wish you could use power to force them to conform, the fact that they are peers actually pushes you toward a healthier, longer-term solution: respectful collaboration. It's not necessarily a bad thing that you feel hesitant or nervous, like you might step on their toes. It forces you to choose your words carefully and speak courteously.

In your conversation, make sure respect is at the forefront. Rather than saying, "You're wrong," say, "I have a different perspective." Instead of, "You messed everything up," try, "Could you explain your thinking here?"

2. ASK REALLY GOOD QUESTIONS.

Since you can't control them, you need to convince them. But you won't convince them until you connect with them, and you won't connect with them until you truly listen to them. In that complicated process, questions are your secret weapon.

This is so much better than showing up with a ten-point list of why you're right and they're wrong. That's only going to make them more defensive, which is a conversation killer. Questions get their brain working in a different direction: either problem-solving (creativity) or personal connection (relationship).

In one Harvard study exploring how question-asking affected people's perception of each other, researchers concluded, "High question-askers—those that probe for information from others—are perceived as more responsive and are better liked."[50] They also concluded that most people don't do this, and instead tend to talk about themselves and promote themselves, adding what we all probably could have guessed: "Our findings suggest that people fail to ask enough questions."

If you're dealing with a complicated coworker, try sprinkling some questions into your conversation: What do you think about this idea? How do you see this problem? Have you ever gone through something like this before? What do you think our goals should be in this situation? What would you suggest here? What dangers do you see?

If you get them talking, they'll often talk themselves right into thinking more highly of you, and that's always a win.

3. NOTICE WHERE YOUR WORLDS COLLIDE.

Another conversation killer is siloed thinking, a.k.a. tunnel vision. This is when everyone sees what matters to them, but they don't really notice other people or departments (other than to complain about them).

If you want to communicate with complicated peers more effectively, try to find places where your worlds intersect and overlap. These are doorways into their day-to-day challenges and environment, and they are a great way to improve your connection. You might need to learn some new terms and concepts here, just as with speaking up to your leadership.

My company once worked with two C-suite executives who just couldn't seem to get on the same page. One was a marketing executive and another was an IT executive. So we helped them explore what they could learn from each other's worlds. The marketing executive needed to better understand the tech world. He needed to be able to speak hardware, software, networks, cybersecurity awareness, data handling, and the cloud. The IT executive needed to better understand the marketing world. She needed to be able to speak design, copywriting, content creation, conversion rates, click-through rates, and customer acquisition costs. When they grew their knowledge base, they even found something they could really connect around: digital marketing tools. Even though they had unique perspectives of these tools, they were both excited about what they could do.

You probably have more in common with that complicated coworker than you think. Use those things as points of connection to develop trust and build bridges.

SPEAKING DOWN
Communicating as a Leader

Regardless of your official title as a leader, when it comes to communication, all leaders are the CRO: the Chief Repeating Officer. I know this is hard to believe, but just because you said it doesn't mean they heard it. Just because it's on your website doesn't mean it's on their mind. And just because it's printed on a wall doesn't mean it's embedded into their behavior.

I'll say it again: CRO is your new title. Tattoo it on your brain. Why? Because if you're going to lead effectively, you are going to have to repeat yourself. A lot. Not because you love to hear your own voice, but because repetition is the golden key to actually getting your message across, especially when you're overseeing complicated employees or direct reports. Sometimes you have to reiterate and restate the same thing over and over again. Repeatedly. Redundantly. Ad infinitum. Ad nauseum.

The best CROs are those who know how to say the same thing in *different ways*. People need to hear things in languages they speak, in terms they understand, and with applications that matter to them. You may fear that will make you sound like a broken record. It won't. Instead, it will make you a good communicator. There's a difference.

By the way, when we looked at the data around how often employees, managers, and executives interacted with complicated people, we noticed that managers tended to report dealing with a higher number of complicated people as well as dealing with complicated people more frequently than employees or executives. This makes sense because managers are in the middle of the org chart. They have to relate to people above, beside, and below them on a regular basis.

If you're a manager, I see your pain. But at least you know you're not alone.

Whether you're an executive, a manager, or anyone else tasked with leading complicated people, the good news is that your downline communication, just like the other directions we've discussed, can be improved with a little intentionality.

This is important when you're casting vision, mission, and values. And it's important when you're setting goals, explaining processes, setting expectations, training new employees, or retraining older ones. But it's especially important when you're navigating complicated topics, such as changes, layoffs, and the dreaded "we're not hitting our targets" talks. These are the kinds of messy conversations that bring out the "complicated" in everyone.

So how do you communicate effectively to a complicated person under your management? And how do you share complicated news with people you lead without causing a riot or having everyone updating their LinkedIn profiles on their phones in the bathroom stalls on their break?

1. KEEP IT REAL.

Don't beat around the bush. Don't spin or sugarcoat things. People have brains and feelings, and they deserve to be treated like it. Whether you're talking about a difficult topic or talking to a difficult person, remember they are intelligent and aware, and treat them accordingly.

In early 2024, Nike was forced to lay off over 1,600 people from their workforce. In a memo sent to employees, CEO John Donahue wrote, "This is a painful reality and not one that I take lightly." He added, "We are not currently performing at our best, and I ultimately hold myself and my leadership team accountable."[51] He kept it real. That's horrible news to have to deliver, and there's no easy way to do it. But there is a clear, respectful, humble way to do it, and that is always the best road to take.

2. KEEP IT SIMPLE.

When you're navigating a thorny topic, don't use so much jargon that it feels like lawyers put it together with a splash of ChatGPT. You don't want people to walk away from the message saying, "So what did they just say?" Whether you're dealing with a challenging topic, person, or both, clarity is your friend.

3. KEEP IT INTERESTING.

Do you know what makes things interesting to people? When they see how it matters to them. Rather than just launching into numbers and charts, tell stories. Show human impact. Connect with people on the level of their motivations. What do they need? What do they want? What are they afraid of? What are they excited about?

4. KEEP IT HOPEFUL.

Give them a light at the end of the tunnel, especially when you're communicating change or asking them to do something they aren't super excited about. Help them see that the current challenge or hardship won't last forever and that their effort, sacrifice, and growth will be worth it.

And remember, at the end of the day, how you treat people might be the greatest message you can send to your team. Your job is to inspire, guide, and sometimes repeat yourself more times than you'd like. Now go out there and communicate like a boss (because, well, you are one).

MEDIUM: USE THE RIGHT TOOLS THE RIGHT WAY

For some people, "tools" instantly conjure up images of saws, drills, and other DIY machinery. Let me be the first to say that I would never attempt a home repair project unless there was an apocalypse and absolutely nobody else was available. Although in that case, home repair would probably not be a priority, so I still wouldn't attempt it. DIY projects are not my thing. Tools are not my love language. I suppose I could fix something if I had to, but the fact of the matter is that I just don't want to. And I'm cool with that.

I do know this, though: there's a right way to use every tool . . . even if I don't know what that is. And if—in some alternate universe—I were planning to build a deck or install a sprinkler system, I would want to know how to use each of those tools.

The same holds true for communication, which is something I'm much more comfortable with. Unlike home repair, communication would be critical during an apocalypse, but that's not my point. My point is that each form of communication has "right" ways to be used. They all have best practices. And there are tips and tricks and hacks to get the most out of them.

It's important to know these things for all communication, but when you're communicating with a complicated individual, they become vital.

While one bursting-at-the-seams chapter in a book isn't enough to cover every medium that exists out there, I want to go through three of the most important communication tools in the workplace:

- **Video calls**
- **Emails**
- **In-person interactions**

Let's start with the most recent addition to the communication toolbox: the infamous video call.

VIDEO CALLS

Nailing Zoom Meetings Without Losing Your Mind (Or Wearing Real Pants)

During the pandemic, the office commute for many people went from avoiding bad drivers on the freeway to avoiding pets and/or small children on the way to the home office (a.k.a. the dining room table), and face-to-face interactions were replaced by Zoom meetings. The pandemic came and went, but video calls are clearly here to stay. Mastering the art of the Zoom (or Webex, or Google Meet, or Microsoft Teams) has become essential to workplace survival.

> **According to our 2024 study, nearly half (44%) of the US workforce work remotely some or all of the time. That's a high number, but it's probably not surprising to anyone. While the traditional workplace is not dead (the other 56% do not work remotely), I don't think anyone can ignore the fact that the landscape is shifting faster than you can say, "You're on mute."**
>
> **This trend is only going to accelerate. A Forbes report in 2023 found that practically every worker out there (98% to be exact) would prefer to work remotely at least some of the time,[52] and I'm certain this universal desire is going to strongly influence employers as they continue filling job roles moving forward.**

What does this mean for you? It means you need to know how to navigate virtual environments. These can be challenging enough on their own, but they get even more difficult when you have difficult individuals on the other side of the screen. Suddenly, you're dealing with complicated people about complicated topics using a complicated tool. So that's fun.

With so many companies now embracing hybrid or fully remote models, let's dive into how you can ace this virtual game.

1. WORK THAT DRESS CODE: PROFESSIONAL(ISH) ON TOP, PARTY ON THE BOTTOM.

Have you ever missed the dress code entirely? I'm still trying to figure out what "business casual" even means. I've logged on suited and booted, only to find a group of Silicon Valley tech execs all wearing hoodies. I spent the first thirty seconds of that meeting deciding if I wanted to own my outfit or pretend like I'd just come from an important in-person meeting. On the other hand, there's nothing like thirty suits and ties looking at you with judgmental eyes as you sit comfortably in a crewneck sweater and Crocs.

I'm not a stylist, but I can say that a three-quarter zip over a collared shirt is undefeated for me. Think news anchor chic—no one needs to know if you're rocking pajama bottoms or (my favorite) Nike basketball shorts.

I realize dress code might not be the first thing that pops into your head when you're thinking about a Zoom call with a complicated person or team, but on a video call, there's not a lot to look at except each other. People are going to be searching for visual clues to either trust or distrust you, so know your audience—and don't show up to a board meeting dressed for a virtual beach party.

Your goals here are to *be appropriate* and *feel confident*. Wearing attire that is appropriate to the meeting builds trust and relatability, and being confident allows you to bring your best self to the meeting. So, in any meeting, but especially in the ones that could be a little dicey, do your dress code homework.

2. KNOW WHEN TO LISTEN AND WHEN TO TALK.

One of the challenges of virtual communication is making sure everyone's voice is heard, including yours. On one hand, it's easy for people to be overlooked or to stay quiet or disengaged in the corner. On the other hand, a few individuals can dominate or interrupt the conversation and end up derailing the meeting.

How you engage with complicated people depends somewhat on whether you are leading the meeting, but regardless of your role, focus on awareness. Try to notice people across the meeting, not only those who are talking. Read their body language (their upper body language, anyway, since that's all you've got to work with). Invite quieter people to speak rather than expecting them to take the initiative. Use tools such as polls and reactions to make sure people are tracking together. Set expectations and rules when it comes to time limits and speaking so nobody gets their feelings hurt. Encourage (or require) people to leave their cameras on, if appropriate.

In virtual environments, active listening can be your superpower. Nodding along, making those "I'm listening" noises, or throwing in a thoughtful question can make all the difference in fostering a collaborative vibe. You are communicating, "I see you, and your ideas matter," without actually saying it.

3. KNOW YOUR PLATFORM.

Know the ins and outs of your virtual platform like the back of your hand—whether it's sharing your screen without sharing your embarrassing browser tabs or using those handy reaction emojis to agree with someone without cutting them off. At the end of the day, your virtual platform is a tool, and that means you can acquire skills at using it. Don't hesitate to ask for help or spend time researching online if you're having trouble.

You need to be able to focus the majority of your attention on people, not the tool. Again, this is always ideal, but it becomes vital when you are on a call with complicated colleagues.

Instead of fighting the virtual medium, work with it. Lean into it. Take advantage of the benefits that a virtual space offers rather than resenting what it doesn't.

4. KEEP YOUR PRESENTATION ENGAGING.

Make your contributions and conversations as engaging as if you were channeling Steve Jobs introducing the iPhone. Be animated, speak confidently, use visuals, throw in an interactive poll, or share a meme that illustrates your point. Remember, in the virtual world, engagement is currency. Your competition is more than simple boredom; it's also the pet knocking over the flowerpot just off-screen or the Amazon delivery guy ringing the doorbell.

Ultimately, mastering your virtual reality is all about being present when you're not, well, present. Part of this comes down to getting the most from your digital platform, as I said above, but a lot of it is about your mindset, body language, and tone. Make people forget they're on the other side of a screen. Keep them so entertained and engaged that they don't notice the glare from their spouse who is taking out the garbage they were supposed to take out last night or the microwave beeping for the umpteenth time because someone forgot they were defrosting dinner.

5. OVERCOMMUNICATE.

While your online colleagues might not recognize you if they ran into you in the supermarket, you can still be memorable and effective by communicating, communicating, communicating. Not in the "spamming Slack at all hours" kind of way, but by keeping your team in the loop on your projects and thoughts. Be the person who brings clarity to chaos, and you'll become as indispensable as the office copier used to be.

This is where digital tools such as Zoom or Teams really shine. You've heard the complaint, "This meeting could have been an email," but video calls can fit in the middle of those two extremes by merging a meeting "feel" with email convenience.

When dealing with complicated people, video offers you the chance to communicate your care, your sincerity, and your humanity in ways that emails and even phone calls can't. The person gets a chance to read your body language and tone, which can be hugely valuable when you're navigating delicate interactions. I know the temptation might be to reduce contact with these people and just fire off short emails or texts, but consider using this tool to engage *more*.

The art of virtual communication is a delicate dance of looking presentable (at least from the waist up), making your virtual presence felt, and not losing your sanity in the process. As we navigate this hybrid work world, remember: flexibility, creativity, and a bit of humor are your best friends.

So wear those superhero pajama bottoms with pride during your next Zoom call, as long as you keep your video cropped appropriately. Here's to thriving in the virtual workspace, one unmuted microphone at a time.

WRITTEN COMMUNICATION
Your Guide to Writing Emails That Others Don't Skim

Most work emails are a snoozefest at best and a confusing mess at worst. It's like everyone suddenly forgets how to communicate the moment they open their email app. But fear not, because crafting emails that don't make your colleagues want to hit "delete" faster than you can say "per my last email" is an art form that anyone can master.

1. LENGTH

First off, brevity is the soul of wit, especially in the inbox. Some folks think they're being helpful by writing a novel, but let's be real: no one has time to read *War and Peace* during work hours. If your email is longer than a TikTok video, you've lost the plot. Get to the point.

On the other hand, don't swing too far and become the master of cryptic one-liners that leave everyone guessing what you actually want. Find the sweet spot—like a perfectly crafted social media post that's short yet informative.

If your email is longer than your average spy novel, consider picking up the phone or walking down the hall. Don't hide behind your screen if what you're trying to convey is better suited for real-time conversation.

2. TONE

Written communication tends to have two built-in dangers. First, it's easier to say negative things when we can't see the reader (hence the toxicity of online interactions). Second, it's all too easy to interpret written communication more negatively than it was intended. Things just look scarier in print. Put those two realities together and you have a recipe for complicated communication.

How do you counteract that? Include some positivity in your email so it doesn't come across grumpier than you meant. And if you're on the receiving end of the email, choose to believe the best about the sender's intentions and seek clarity if you're not sure.

Also, be aware that fears and frustrations have a way of sneaking into the wording we use, similar to body language and tone when we're speaking. It's not *what* we're writing but *how* we write it. Consider the following example:

Subject: Project deadline reminder

Dear Team,

As I'm sure you're all aware, the deadline for our project is next Friday. I've noticed that some of you have yet to submit your parts. While I understand we're all busy, it's important to remember that everyone's work is crucial to the project's success. Let's try to meet our deadlines moving forward.

Best, [Your Name]

This email is polite and professional on the surface, but did you catch the undercurrent of frustration and blame? If you were on the receiving end of it, you'd feel like you were being called out, or you'd wonder which of your team members was screwing up the whole thing, or you'd think your boss was just being their grouchy self again. Here's a slightly revised version of the same email.

> Subject: Support for project completion
>
> Dear Team,
> I hope this message finds you well. With our project deadline approaching next Friday, I wanted to offer my support to anyone needing assistance with their sections. I understand we're all managing various responsibilities, and I appreciate everyone's hard work and dedication to making this project a success. If you're facing any challenges or if there's anything I can do to help, please don't hesitate to reach out.
>
> Warm regards, [Your Name]

There is still some urgency and accountability there, but instead of accusing people in a passive-aggressive way, it offers support. Rather than being alienating, it's collaborative. And instead of highlighting individual failures, it focuses on team success.

There are many statements that can give a negative vibe. You've probably been triggered by a few of these.

INSTEAD OF

"I haven't heard back from my last email." → "I understand emails can sometimes be overlooked; may I ask for an update on this?"

"Not sure if you noticed, but . . . " → "I wanted to highlight / bring to your attention . . . "

"Just a friendly reminder . . . " → "I'm following up on . . . "

"I'm not sure if this was your intention, but . . . " → "I noticed a discrepancy that we might need to discuss . . . "

"It's fine, I'll do it myself." → "I understand this might be challenging; how can we address this together?"

"For future reference, we typically . . . " → "As a best practice, we usually . . . . This helps ensure consistency and quality."

You're not typing on eggshells. You're simply being considerate of what it's like to be on the other side of an email from you.

3. PERSONALITY

Now, on to the personality crisis plaguing most work emails. Yes, it's work, but that doesn't mean you have to sound like a robot programmed to bore people to death. Injecting a little personality doesn't mean littering your text with emojis (please don't), or ending every sentence with exclamation marks (please don't!!), or stalking someone's social media to comment on their weekend activities (a little creepy), but it does mean letting a bit of your human side show through, and it means acknowledging the recipient as a human being. A little warmth goes a long way in not making emails feel like they're coming from the corporate overlord. A simple "Hope you had a great weekend" or "Congrats on wrapping up that big project" can transform your email from "mark as read" to actually read.

4. CLARITY

Clarity is your best friend. If there's one thing worse than a boring email, it's an email that leaves you more confused than when you started reading it. Don't assume everyone's inside your head. Be clear about what you want, why you want it, and when you want it by. And for the love of all that is efficient, bullet points are your allies. They're a shortcut to clarity and conciseness, so use them liberally.

Someone once said, "It's not enough to write so that you can be understood—you should write so that you cannot be misunderstood." I couldn't agree more. Consider how your message will be received, particularly by complicated people, and focus on making yourself clear.

Writing emails is about human-level connection and communication, not screaming your message into the digital void and hoping recipients get the point. Communicate your message in an efficient, effective *length* and use a positive, respectful *tone.* Throw in a touch of *personality,* and ensure *clarity.*

IN-PERSON INTERACTIONS:
Conversation for the Rest of Us

While COVID-19 taught us how to use Zoom better, it worked against us when it comes to in-person connections. A 2023 survey of over 1,500 business leaders found that more than six out of ten companies were planning to offer etiquette training by 2024, covering topics such as making polite conversation, dressing professionally, writing emails, and making eye contact.[53]

Elaine Swann, founder of The Swann School of Protocol, says that when people were working from home, "The soft skills that are necessary to have a harmonious workplace were not being used. . . . Utilizing those skills is almost like a muscle. If you're not using that muscle, it can become weak."[54]

Across the workplace, the post-pandemic world needs to get its manners back. Of course, even before the pandemic, these topics weren't necessarily easy. And some of us struggle more than others. I'm an introvert, as I mentioned earlier. Some people find that surprising given what I do for a living, which is speaking in front of thousands of people, sometimes multiple times a week. For me, speaking to a crowd is much easier and less draining than that dreaded monster: small talk.

I've had to work at becoming a conversationalist. Odds are, you have too. Even if you're by nature an extrovert, you've had to hone your skills at in-person interactions, starting as soon as you could talk.

Despite the prevalence of digital meetings and email, many of us still spend a fair amount of time each week in the actual, physical presence of people we work with.

THAT MEANS WE HAVE TO GROW OUR SOCIAL SKILLS "MUSCLES" IF WE WANT TO EFFECTIVELY CONNECT AND WORK WITH OTHERS.

Specifically, we need to learn how to:

1. USE SMALL TALK TO BUILD TRUST EQUITY

Humans are social creatures. We build trust one interaction at a time. That means every hallway interaction is a chance to strengthen your connection with people you might struggle with a little, such as those complicated ones we've been talking about.

You don't have to be the life of the party, but you shouldn't be all business either. Instead of viewing casual conversations as a distraction or chore, use them to build trust equity with complicated people by connecting over small things—weather, sports, the quality (or lack thereof) of the cafeteria food. Then, when trickier issues arise, you have at least a footbridge of connection.

If small talk is a big problem for you, here are some suggestions:

- **HAVE SOME CONVERSATION STARTERS IN YOUR BACK POCKET**
  Rely on go-to topics such as current events or whatever sports team is doing well in your city.

- **ASK OPEN-ENDED QUESTIONS.**
  "What did you do this weekend?" or "What are your hobbies?" Get them talking and take the pressure off yourself.

- **MICRODOSE YOUR OWN LIFE STORY.**
 Don't overshare, but also don't be afraid to mention things from your past or personal life that make you more relatable.

- **EMBRACE THE PAUSE.**
 Not every moment has to be filled with words.

- **ACCEPT YOUR PERSONALITY.**
 Your introverted qualities, like thoughtfulness and observation, can make you a great conversationalist. You don't have to dominate the conversation to be engaging.

- **DON'T OVERTHINK THIS.**
 People probably think about you less than you think they do, and they don't walk around all day remembering that joke you tried to tell that fell flat. Relax, be friendly, and have fun.

2. CRACK THE CODE OF BODY LANGUAGE

Body language refers to the nonverbal ways we communicate. It includes facial expressions, gestures, postures, movements, eye contact, personal space, touch, and (at least by some definitions) the tone and volume of your voice.

Experts estimate that these cues account for 60–70% of human communication, and research has shown that nonverbal messages are usually more believable than verbal ones,[55] meaning that if what I say with my mouth doesn't match what I say with my body, others will tend to believe my body.

How many of these nonverbal cues can you instantly recognize and interpret?

- Frown
- Smile
- Shrug
- Wink
- Scowl
- Crossed arms
- Thumbs-up
- Eye roll
- Hands on hips

- Fidgeting
- Nod
- Yawn
- Leaning in
- Leaning back
- Raised eyebrows
- Pursed lips
- Clenched fists
- Widened eyes

You could probably visualize every single one of these immediately. We instinctively pick up on other people's thoughts and feelings by reading "the quiet part," the part they don't say out loud but broadcast through their body language.

In essence, we're reading their minds. That's a superpower, if we can learn to do it well.

In high-stress moments, it's easy to forget about body language. For example, if you're giving an important presentation or pitch, force yourself to slow down and read the people in the room, then respond accordingly. If they look defensive, scared, or confused, don't just plow ahead with what you planned to say. Pivot. Ask questions. Address concerns. Get them on the same page before you keep going, or you might as well stop right then. Either they are not listening or they're arguing with you in their heads, and neither of those is healthy communication.

You can also use body language to your advantage. Again, the key is awareness. When you're having a difficult conversation with a complicated person, pay attention to what you are communicating through your stance, your expressions, and your gestures. Do you look closed? Aggressive? Doubtful? Angry? Worried? Discouraged?

While you can't really "fake" body language, at least for long, you can make sure your body aligns with the approach you want to have. Try uncrossing your arms, smiling, relaxing your face, talking slower, widening your eyes, opening your stance, nodding, and anything else that communicates openness and collaboration.

3. REMEMBER THAT MANNERS MATTER

Young children may see good manners and proper etiquette as simply following made-up rules, but adults (should) know better. They are about showing respect to people by acting in appropriate ways.

Appropriate is the key word here. For example, you're practically expected to yell and scream at a basketball game, but you wouldn't do that in a restaurant, even though there isn't a sign on the wall that says "No Yelling." Why? At some point, probably as a toddler, you were taught that it's inappropriate and disrespectful.

Similarly, when you're talking to people at work, there are unspoken, unwritten rules of conduct that help us all get along. These vary from culture to culture, from company to company, and from team to team, which means you need to pay attention. The questions you're trying to answer are: *What is considered respectful?* and *What is considered appropriate?*

While good manners are important for everyone, they are especially important when dealing with complicated people for two reasons: first, because these people are more likely to get under your skin and make you forget your manners; and second, because they're more likely to get offended or upset if you disrespect them.

Here are a few tips to help you have good conversational manners:

- **MAINTAIN EYE CONTACT WHEN YOU TALK TO SOMEONE.**

  Don't keep checking your phone or your watch, and don't stare off into the distance.

- **DON'T INTERRUPT.**

  This is a big one. If you can't let someone finish what they're saying, why are you even talking to them? Apparently, you already know everything . . . or at least that's what they'll think about you.

- **AVOID MAKING COMMENTS OR JOKES THAT ARE BELITTLING, RUDE, OR VULGAR.**
  Keep things professional.

- **USE PEOPLE'S NAMES.**
  (And pronounce and spell them correctly!) Everyone loves to hear their own name.

- **REMEMBER THEIR ROLE.**
  Even if you are friends, people's position, authority, and title usually matter to them. You don't have to grovel, but don't be so chummy that you cross a line.

- **LISTEN MORE THAN YOU TALK.**
  Be aware of the balance and focus of the conversation, and intentionally turn the topic toward other people.

Whether you're on a Zoom call with someone across the world, composing an email to a challenging colleague, or chatting it up in the hallway at work, the way you communicate matters. Pick the right tool for the job, then use it the right way.

And remember, direction matters. Are you speaking up? Down? Across? Pay attention to the dynamics and complexities of your relationships.

There's a Spanish proverb that says, *Cada cabeza es un mundo,* which means, "Every head is a world." It's usually used when someone just did something baffling. It's a way of saying, "I have no idea why they did that, but I guess it made sense to them."

But why settle for that? You have a toolbox full of ways to peer inside other people's heads. If you focus on communicating, I believe you can find effective ways to connect and collaborate with (nearly) anyone.

So far, we've talked about working with complicated colleagues who are up (such as bosses and owners), down (those who report to you), and across (peers).

Next, we're going to look at one more complicated direction:

CHAPTER 9

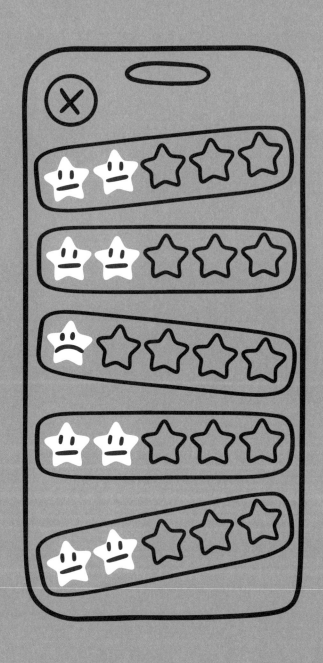

THE CUSTOMER IS NOT ALWAYS RIGHT

Let's get one thing straight: the customer is *not* always right. Neither is the patient, the client, the subscriber, the user, the fan, the passenger, the patron, the member, or the follower.

The customer who insists that "unlimited breadsticks" means you should cater their wedding for free is not always right. The patient who self-diagnosed their illness via Google is not always right. The passenger who believes they should be allowed to bring their emotional support peacock on the flight is not always right.

Nevertheless, these are people who buy your products, use your services, or consume your creative content, and you've been taught to respect and accommodate them at the cost of your time, your energy, and sometimes even your sanity.

There are all kinds of complicated people you will come across whom you're supposed to accommodate. The list is endless, but here are a few. See how many of these you recognize from your own experience:

- **The Perfectionist:** This is the person who would give Mother Teresa a two-star review.

- **The Worrier:** This is the client who panic-texts you at ten p.m. because they just thought of an even worse worst-case scenario than the one they texted you about at eight p.m.

- **The Ghost:** This is the person who asks for multiple rounds of detailed estimates and then vanishes forever.

- **The Cheapskate:** This is the client who expects a spaceship on a tricycle budget.

- **The Know-It-All:** This is the person who thinks your education and experience cannot possibly be more accurate than their uninformed but loudly proclaimed opinion.

- **The Overthinker:** This is the client who needs a committee to choose a coffee flavor.

- **The Catastrophizer:** This is the person who turns minor setbacks into Shakespearean tragedies.

- **The Rookie:** This is the client who thinks SEO is a new diet fad.

- **The Procrastinator:** This is the guy who sends you urgent emails marked "reply ASAP" after weeks of radio silence.

- **The Fighter:** This is the person who can turn any agreement into an argument.

- **The Bully:** This is the customer who treats every interaction as a chance to boost their ego at the expense of yours.

- **The Pessimist:** This is the customer who sees a dark cloud around every silver lining.

- **The Traditionalist:** This is the client who thinks humanity peaked in the 1980s and it's all been downhill from there.

THE WILD WORLD OF CUSTOMER SERVICE

Where did we get the idea that we have to bend over backward to accommodate every complicated customer or client? This concept has been around for quite a while, actually.

The phrase "the customer is always right" was popularized by retail tycoons like Harry Gordon Selfridge, John Wanamaker, and Marshall Field in the early twentieth century. Swiss hotelier César Ritz, of Ritz-Carlton fame, had a similar slogan: *Le client n'a jamais tort* ("The customer is never wrong").[56] These early entrepreneurs revolutionized customer service by putting the customer's needs and satisfaction at the forefront of their business model. This philosophy worked well in a time when consumer choices were limited and customer loyalty was built through exceptional service.

Fast-forward to today, when customers are like toddlers hyped up on sugar: demanding, unpredictable, and prone to tantrums. Do we really need to keep everyone happy all the time and at any cost? In a world where one bad Yelp review can cause a business to implode, is that even possible? Maybe it's time to reconsider how we work with the complicated people we serve, sell to, teach, and entertain.

Regardless of your industry or role, you probably find yourself engaged in outward-facing interactions with complicated people on a regular basis.

There are two really good reasons to get better at working with complicated clients and customers: first, because there are a lot of them out there. According to our research, customers and clients are the second-highest source of complicated individuals for US workers, with 55% of people highlighting this area. The top source was peers, at 66%. All the other categories (managers, direct reports, and executives) ranked much lower.

The second reason is even more important: because your business depends on them. When we quizzed people about how they tended to handle complicated customers and clients using the four strategies we discussed earlier—ignore them, change them, cancel them, or understand them—we found that the vast majority of respondents try to understand them. Interestingly, they chose this strategy more often with customers and clients than with anyone else they worked with, including their peers. In other words, we try even harder to understand customers than we do our coworkers.

That makes sense, doesn't it? The people we're talking about here are your job security. They are the ones you depend on for the livelihood of your company, which means they hold a lot of power in the relationship. You can't tick them off, blow them off, or write them off because your business exists *for them*.

But they can be *so stinking complicated*. If you don't know how to deal with them, you can feel trapped in a lose-lose scenario. You either put up with their demands or you lose their business. Neither feels like a good option.

Here's the thing, though. If you've actually worked with customers, you know they sometimes *are* wrong. They have wrong facts, wrong attitudes, wrong expectations, and wrong behavior. They can even be abusive, sexist, racist, and toxic.

So what can you do?

YOU CAN START RETHINKING HOW YOU SEE CUSTOMER SERVICE.

I'm always fascinated by stories of companies who have rethought customer service. Walt Disney was one of the best, of course. Disney's ongoing commitment to providing excellent service to every one of their millions of annual visitors is legendary. In his book *Customer Rules*, Lee Cockerell, who served as Executive Vice President of Operations at Walt Disney World, writes,

> **IN TODAY'S HIGHLY COMPETITIVE** marketplace, a business needs more than excellent products, good technical service, efficient procedures, and more competitive prices to win customers. It also needs to truly connect with its customers through authentic, human-to-human interactions that satisfy not only their practical needs, but their emotional wants.[57]

I love his holistic focus here. Customers are people, and people have both "practical needs" and "emotional wants." Both are important, especially when we're dealing with the challenging souls we're calling *complicated*.

There are countless other companies who have gained fame for their exceptional ability to serve customers. Ritz-Carlton, Nordstrom, Zappos, Neiman-Marcus, and Chick-fil-A are a few that come to mind. They may differ on their policies and procedures, but they agree on one thing: they want to provide excellent service to every single client or customer—*especially* the complicated ones.

That's precisely what makes these companies stand out, isn't it? And it's what can make *you* stand out too. Anyone can be nice to nice people, but how you deal with the complicated ones is the litmus test of your customer service skills. Can you keep your cool and work to find solutions even when you're confronted with the dark side of people? Or for that matter, when you see the human side? Things like stress, ignorance, defensiveness, frustration, selfishness, and impatience are part and parcel of being human.

DON'T CALL PEOPLE DEMONS JUST BECAUSE THEY DON'T ACT LIKE ANGELS; THEY'RE SIMPLY HUMANS.

SO, HOW CAN YOU GET BETTER AT INTERACTING AND COLLABORATING WITH THESE PEOPLE?

HOW TO WORK WITH COMPLICATED CUSTOMERS

All the principles we've looked at in this book can be applied to customers and clients, but let me give you a few that are specifically focused on customer service, especially when the customer you're serving is complicated.

1. SURPRISE THEM WITH KINDNESS

Rather than getting defensive when people are bad-tempered or ill-mannered, go on the offensive by being nice. The bar is often set so low for customer service that all you have to do is let your human decency show a little, and you'll deescalate the situation in the short-term and win their loyalty in the long-term.

I'll never forget the day I was out with my children at a kids' event. We were hungry, so we walked up to one of the food trucks that was on-site. The woman taking our order had the biggest smile in the world. The cook, though, was peeved. He hated his life, his job, and probably me because I represented three more people he had to cook for. And I'm not going to lie—our order was crazy complicated. So in this story, I'm the complicated customer for sure. Plus, we were starving, so we ordered way too much food.

The cook mumbled something to the cashier. I couldn't hear what he said, which was probably a good thing. But she kept her contagious smile and replied, "Hey, it's going to be alright."

We ended up waiting a solid twenty-five minutes for food that should have taken maybe seven minutes to prepare. I was getting a little impatient, even upset. But when I walked over to check on the food, the cashier had the same huge, authentic smile on her face. It disarmed me completely. I walked back to the kids, shrugged, and said, "It's okay. We can wait."

What did that woman do? She realized, in a stressful situation, *This customer is complicated. My coworker is too. But how I treat people is my choice, and it makes a difference.*

She refused to get defensive when I got impatient, and she refused to catch her coworker's bad attitude. Instead, she lent us her smile and calm demeanor, which I then passed on to my kids. Imagine if she would have snarled at me instead of smiling at me. The story would have had a different ending because all of us would have been hating life, each other, and food trucks in general.

I don't know if she changed her coworker's mood, but she changed mine. That's the power of knowing how to deal with complicated people in complicated situations. In this case, the customer wasn't easy and my attitude wasn't great, but I was still human, and she never lost sight of that. Instead of seeing a grumpy customer, she saw a hungry parent wrangling two cranky kids.

Regardless of your industry or role, consider how you could be proactively nice to people. Make a game of it. Challenge yourself to find creative ways to surprise people with generous, helpful action, and short-circuit their crankiness with your kindness.

No, it won't always work, at least not if you define "working" as turning a complicated person into an easy person. But that's not the goal, remember? You're focusing on collaboration, and collaboration is always a work in progress. Kindness will *always* improve collaboration, even if it only improves how you experience the interaction (which is all you can control anyway).

Besides, what's your other option? Surprise them with nastiness? Match their level of grumpiness? You can never beat negativity with more negativity. Kindness is always a better choice.

2. FIND THE GIFT IN THEIR GRUMPY

All criticism is constructive if you take it right. It either helps you see where you're wrong, or it helps you reaffirm where you're right. Each is a gift.

However, when you are first given negative feedback, you're usually going to assume the feedback is wrong and you are right. That's just human nature. You won't know if you need to change until you move past the initial emotional reaction and dissect the feedback humbly and objectively. This requires making a conscious choice to say no to defensiveness and yes to curiosity.

Negative feedback is invaluable. You should ask for it. You should be willing to pay for it. But make sure that *in your heart* you value the people who are willing to speak up for what they think is important. Do you really want to surround yourself with people who think just like you do? That's called living in a bubble, and it's inherently dangerous. You need prickly people to come along and pop the bubble.

Even if nothing needs to change in your product or service, maybe something needs to change in your communication. How can you set the right expectations—and then exceed them?

Of course, the customer always *thinks* they're right, but that doesn't *make* them right. Just because they said it doesn't make it true. In order to effectively evaluate criticism, you need to know how much weight to give different people's opinions.

For example, if my wife tells me I need to change something, I'm going to pay a lot more attention than if someone I don't even know criticizes me in an Instagram comment. It's not that those voices on social media don't matter. They might have something to teach me, and I do care about them—but they don't get the same access to my emotions or choices as my wife does.

Brené Brown recommends having what she calls a "square squad."[58] On a one-inch square piece of paper, write down the names of the people whose opinions truly matter to you. The point of making it so small is that it forces you to edit. Then make sure you're listening primarily to those people.

Too often, we have an "everyone squad." We have the name of every friend, customer, employee, and social media troll all scribbled on there. But some of them just don't deserve that much attention.

Make sure you're listening to the people who genuinely care for you and will tell you the truth—not just about your weaknesses, but also about your strengths. Don't let unfounded criticism derail your dream or shift your core principles. Instead, pay the most attention to the voices that matter the most.

Go ahead and listen to grumpy feedback, and then thank the person for their honesty (if appropriate). Then analyze it objectively, discard whatever is bad, and hold on to whatever is good.

3. DON'T LET *WHERE* YOU WORK DETERMINE *HOW* YOU WORK

The other day on a road trip, I took my family to a Buc-ee's. If you've never been to one, you need to put it on your bucket list.

Here's what you need to know about Buc-ee's: it's a gas station and a convenience store. The thing is, apparently nobody in the company's management knows that gas stations and convenience stores are places you only go to out of necessity, leave as fast as possible, and definitely don't expect much from in the way of customer service.

Buc-ee's is the exact opposite. They are enormous, well-stocked, organized, and clean. The restrooms have hand sanitizer dispensers in every stall so no one has an excuse not to wash their hands. The line of gas pumps is so long you can hardly see the end. They literally hold the world record for the largest convenience store (75,593 square feet, in Luling, Texas) and longest car wash (255 feet, in Katy, Texas).[59]

I took my family to a Buc-ee's on the way home from a vacation, where we had stayed in a five-star resort. We got treated better at this gas station than at the resort. I'm not exaggerating. At least a dozen Buc-ee's employees had greeted us by the time we got to the counter to check out.

Now, think about their customers: *people who are driving*. Can you think of a more complicated customer base than stressed-out drivers and exhausted families? Yet somehow they've managed to make their gas station an oasis to enjoy rather than a torment to endure.

My kids walked out of Buc-ee's with more merch than they did at the theme park we'd gone to. I wasn't even sure why at the time, but now I get it: it's because Buc-ee's exceeded our expectations.

Granted, that wasn't difficult, considering the quality of many gas stations. But still, they didn't have to go *that* hard. They chose to. They didn't settle for the industry standard. They didn't match the energy of the customers who dragged their tired selves onto the premises. They didn't let *where* they worked determine *how* they worked.

Maybe you don't work for a *company* that does that, but *you* can still do that. What is stopping you from bringing your best self to every interaction? Even if you don't work at the Ritz-Carlton, you can still carry yourself with grace, class, and excellence.

If you lead a team or company, challenge yourself to build a culture that makes people shake their head in awe. Don't settle for the industry standard. *Set* the industry standard.

4. DON'T GET MAD; GET CREATIVE

I actually like Mr. Ritz's phrase *Le client n'a jamais tort* ("The customer is never wrong") better than "The customer is always right." Customers are not always right, but they're not necessarily wrong either. They have genuine needs, frustrations, and concerns. They might not be right about how to address them, but that doesn't mean they are wrong to have them. Put another way, their feelings might not be justified, but they are still valid. They are humans, after all, and humans get all up in their feels on a regular basis.

Good customer service requires you to meet people where they are, in a nonjudgmental way, and figure out what you can do about their needs and concerns. At the end of the day, most cranky customers just want solutions. Sure, there is a subset who are looking for an excuse to complain, but I think the majority of the complicated people you deal with would be a lot less complicated if you could find a way to meet their immediate felt need.

The problem is that the solution they demand often doesn't jibe with the reality they're living in. And since nobody has figured out how to teleport to alternate universes yet, you're stuck trying to get them to settle for less than what they want. That's a setup for disappointment.

Unfortunately, sometimes that is all you can do. Maybe bad weather grounded a flight, and you have a line of angry passengers in front of you. Or maybe your restaurant's freezer failed and all the meat spoiled, leaving a dining room full of hungry customers unserved. Or maybe a car part got lost in transit and you can't get a customer's repair done in time. Sometimes you just can't fix things the way you wish you could.

So what can you do? Get creative. Maybe there is an alternate way to get them the solution they want, or maybe there is an alternate solution that's different than what they want but still meets their needs. When it comes to customer service, solutions are generally more effective than apologies.

THIS REQUIRES LISTENING AND TIME.

Both of those are sadly often lacking in customer service because we're rushing to get so much done. If you're going to come up with a creative solution, you're going to have to really understand what the person is frustrated about and why. Once you see things from their point of view, you can often leverage your greater knowledge and experience to offer ideas that neither of you would have thought of before.

One of my clients who runs the concierge service for a high-end fitness club told me about a particular customer who became extremely irate over an issue with guest passes. He was making a scene at the front desk, saying that because he was paying $300 a month, he should be able to bring whoever he wanted, whenever he wanted, to the club. The man refused to listen to the manager's explanation and began talking over her and trying to embarrass and intimidate her right there at the front desk.

She brought him into her office, sat him down, and said, "Help me understand what's going on." He explained that his sister-in-law and her daughter were visiting from out of the country for almost two months, and he wanted them to be able to use the gym.

The manager said she understood, and while she couldn't get them guest passes for that long, she could set the sister-in-law up with a membership of her own. As they talked, though, she discovered that the reason he'd brought up the money issue in the first place was because his wife was battling breast cancer and she wasn't even using the gym. The conflict with the guest passes wasn't just an issue of policy for the man; there was an emotional component that needed to be unpacked.

The manager was able to refund the wife's portion of the membership, and the man walked out with money in his bank account, a membership for his sister-in-law, and, most importantly, the feeling of having been listened to and understood.

The customer wasn't exactly right, but he wasn't totally wrong either. All it took to change his attitude was a manager who was willing to listen and able to think creatively.

Often, the most important need isn't just the superficial thing people are arguing with you about, especially if you both know the problem is unsolvable. Maybe they need to be heard. Maybe they need to express themselves. Maybe they need to feel valued. Maybe they need another human to acknowledge and care about their frustration. And since you work for the company that they're frustrated with, they want to tell you what they wish they could tell the company.

They are not wrong to want that. Maybe you can't fix the issue . . . but maybe you don't need to. Maybe they simply need someone at the company to listen and care, and you're the one they're looking at. Lucky you.

That doesn't mean you have to be a punching bag for them to take out their frustrations, but it does mean you need to practice a high level of emotional intelligence during the encounter. Remember that you're not just listening to them rant; you're meeting a need they have to be heard. That's invaluable.

They know you can't control the weather, but the fact that you care deeply that they're going to miss a family funeral might be all they need. They know you can't magically whip up a meal unless they're okay with going vegetarian for an hour, but your genuine apology and a good restaurant recommendation can go a long way. They know the car part is stuck on a ship somewhere and it's out of your hands, but your honesty and compassion (and maybe a loaner car) might turn their mood around.

If you can meet their needs creatively—even if they're just psychological ones—people will often walk away in a different mood than when they arrived. Remember that smiling lady in the food truck? Her customer service transcended her environment, and it was contagious. I don't remember much about the food, and the twenty-five-minute wait is water under the bridge, but I won't easily forget her grace and excellence.

How about you? Do you have any complicated customers, clients, guests, visitors, patients, followers, viewers, users, consumers, or anyone else? I'm sure you do. I certainly do, too, and I know I'll have many more in the days and years to come.

How will we engage with those complicated people? Will we match their frustration? Or will we meet it with kindness, humility, grace, and creativity?

Nobody else gets to decide that for you, my friend. Not the grumpy customer, not your company, not your boss, not your coworker, not anyone. The customer is not always right—but you can still treat them right. That choice is always in your hands.

The customer is not always right, and the same could be said for any complicated person you work with. They are often wrong in their perspective, their attitude, their tone, their demands, their reactions, and their habits, which is precisely what makes them complicated. We need to address an important but uncomfortable caveat, though: sometimes complicated people *actually are right*—or at least they are not totally wrong. If we're going to effectively collaborate with them, we have to listen to the complexities and nuance of their complicated *messages* rather than simply shooting the complicated *messenger*. In other words, we will need to get better at dealing with disagreements and conflict, which is what we're going to examine in the following chapter.

CHAPTER 10

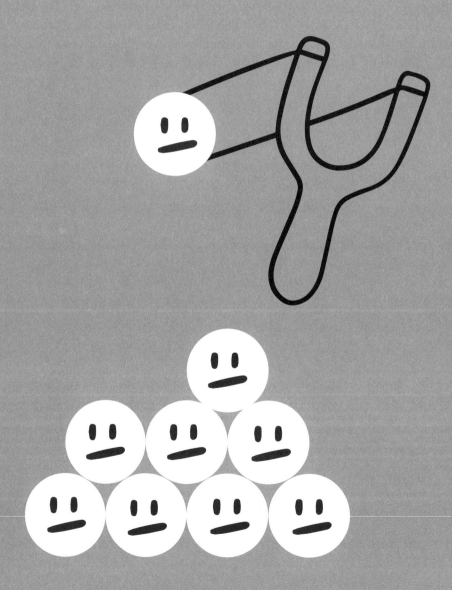

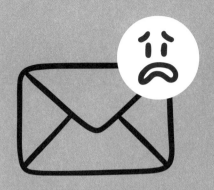

DON'T SHOOT THE MESSENGER

People be lying.

That's what I've learned working with hundreds of organizations over the last decade. *People be lying* all the time.

They have their reasons for it. They like health insurance, and they believe the truth could make them lose it. They like direct deposits, and the truth could make every other Friday a lot more anxious.

But one of the biggest reasons people lie is that they don't believe the person they're talking to can actually handle the truth. They're afraid the wrong words or an unwelcome truth will start a war, and they aren't really in the mood to be on the receiving end of that.

So instead of saying what they want to say or need to say, they tiptoe around the truth. They spin things and hide things. They avoid conflict or hide from disagreements rather than facing them head-on.

But when the truth is sacrificed to "not make the boss mad" or "keep so-and-so from quitting," everyone loses.

I remember one C-suite leader telling me with a straight face that everyone around her loved their jobs. That's what they always said, and that's what she always believed.

When I told her that probably wasn't entirely true, she was shocked. "But why would they lie?" she asked.

"Why wouldn't they lie?" I replied. "They need their paycheck."

Many leaders cannot fathom a world where the people who work for them would lie to them. But you have to remember, people are smart, and they need to survive. If they tell you the truth, and if that reflects poorly on your leadership, they know it might not end well for them. So they bite their tongues and say what you want to hear, then go back to surfing job websites when your back is turned.

So . . . can you handle the truth? That's the question you need to ask yourself. Especially when the person delivering the information is a bit complicated. Especially when the "facts" (according to them) challenge our assumptions or require us to make hard choices. Especially when the "truth" (again, according to them) doesn't mesh with the "truth" according to us. What happens when my truth and your truth are on a collision course?

In those moments, it's tempting to insulate ourselves from unwelcome debates and uncomfortable opinions. It's all too easy to label the bearer of bad tidings "complicated" and then shoot the messenger.

Consider the tragic tale of BlackBerry. Do you remember BlackBerry phones? I had one back in the early 2000s when I was working at a cell phone kiosk in a mall. Before iPhone and Android phones took the world by storm, BlackBerry owned the smartphone market.

Honestly, they pretty much created the market.

It started in 2002 when a Canadian pager company named Research in Motion (RIM) built one of the world's first smartphones. They called it the BlackBerry. It had a full keyboard and email connectivity, and the business world fell in love with it. Suddenly, executives and salespeople were no longer tethered to their desks. They could send emails from their boardroom, bedroom, bathroom, or anywhere else. Within four years, RIM hit annual sales of $10 billion.

Then, in 2007, the iPhone exploded onto the market, followed soon after by Google's Android-based phone.

And BlackBerry did . . . nothing. At least not until it was too late.

Their revenue was still growing, after all. They were convinced they owned the business market, and these newcomers with their "fun" phones and third-party apps were for nonbusiness consumers. When they finally realized they were being beaten at their own game, they responded slowly and ineffectively. Their "answer" to the iPhone, the ill-fated BlackBerry Storm, was a colossal failure that tanked their reputation even further. Five years later, they lost $70 billion in market value, and their share of the market shrank to a tiny fraction. It was a spectacular fall from power for the company that had helped crack open Pandora's box of smartphones.

Why didn't they respond faster? One problem was a lack of diversity of thought. In 2012, shortly after both of RIM's co-CEOs resigned under pressure from investors, an article by CBS MoneyWatch stated, "All eight of RIM's outside directors, including its chairman and lead director, are accountants, economists, and finance people." The writer added, "Like minds think alike and are subject to group-think."[60]

The term *groupthink* is a concept from psychology that describes how groups can unintentionally "force" sameness of thought among themselves by valuing harmony so highly that they squash dissenting voices. It's basically mass self-deception. It's death by lack of diversity.

Ever been there? Have you ever seen the dissenting voice in the room or Zoom be squashed? The reality is that we need diversity of thought. We need differences of opinion. And that means we probably need to let a few complicated people share their complicated opinions, even if they make us uncomfortable.

Essentially, the decision-makers at RIM told themselves they were right—and then believed themselves. That's fairly common human behavior, if we're being honest. One BlackBerry insider later said, "The problem wasn't that we stopped listening to customers. We believed we knew better what customers needed long term than they did."[61]

The way RIM responded to shifting market trends is the polar opposite of Mr. William Wrigley of chewing gum fame. Wrigley's willingness to listen to employees who disagreed with him, and his ability to rethink his products and strategy based on customer feedback, are two sides of the same coin: he cared about what was true, not just what was comfortable, so he was able to cut his losses, pivot, and seize new opportunities.

His success didn't come from never making a mistake or misreading the market, because he did both. It came, at least in part, because he listened to people—customers and employees—who contradicted his opinions and upended his plans.

THAT LEVEL OF HUMILITY IS BOTH INSPIRING AND RARE.

DEALING WITH DISAGREEMENTS

If you want to collaborate effectively with complicated people, make peace with conflict. That sounds like an oxymoron, but it's true. Disagreements are going to come along, and you need to be prepared to handle them.

One large international study by CPP, the company behind the Myers-Briggs Type Indicator, found that the average employee spends over two hours a week dealing with workplace conflict. In the US, that works out to 385 million workdays per year spent on conflict.[62]

Noticed I said "spent" on conflict, not "wasted." In and of itself, conflict is not bad. It's not good either. It just is. It's a fact of life and a reality of working with people.

What makes conflict good or bad primarily comes down to:

(a) how you handle it, and

(b) what you get from it.

"How you handle it" is mostly about emotional intelligence, which we looked at earlier. Can you disagree with someone elegantly, gracefully, and maturely? Or does every argument turn into a shouting match or an ego duel? Or, just as bad, do you simply shut up and shut down?

> **Most of us think we're pretty good at this. In our survey, 73% of working Americans say they typically respond well when someone at work provides them with constructive feedback in an area in which they need to improve. Executives were even more confident: 81% of them graded themselves highly here. But . . . do three out of four people you know respond well to criticism?**

I suspect this is one of those areas where we look at ourselves as angelic and everyone else as problematic. If we're honest, I think we could all admit that sometimes we respond well, and sometimes we respond not so well. There is always room for improvement.

"What you get from it" is about outcomes. Do you use disagreements to move you forward? Do you debate and discuss and disagree until answers are discovered? Or do you end arguments prematurely to "keep the peace," even if that means settling for mediocrity or failure?

Healthy disagreement is a necessary part of progress. You can't expect to move forward without some conflicts along the way, and conflict that is properly managed will naturally move you forward. Disagreement is a tool to use, not a problem to avoid.

We have to make a conscious choice to adopt this mindset because many of us are driven by a desire for either peace or productivity, and both of those get interrupted by conflicts among colleagues.

The interruption is temporary, though. That's helpful to keep in mind when tensions are rising and ideas are clashing. Ultimately, if you don't have the courage or time to debate crucial issues, you'll wind up sabotaging both your peace and your productivity. Pressure will build up until it blows up, and then you'll be left to clean up.

In light of the obvious value of diverse thinking, it's a bit sobering to consider how often the label "complicated person" is applied to people who are willing to speak up when others are silent. Just because someone asks hard questions or has unpopular opinions does not make them wrong, and it does not make them complicated.

IT MAKES THEM VALUABLE.

Mark, a friend who leads a Fortune 100 company, shared with me a story about a personality test he and a number of his leaders took. A consultant with the company administering the test sat down afterward with Mark and told him that he and two other top-level leaders had the same personality: driven, results-oriented, and efficient. But another key leader on the team, a guy we'll call Richard, was different. He was more empathetic and feelings-oriented.

The consultant told Mark that based on their styles, he could guess what their meeting dynamics were like. If the three driver-type leaders were the only ones in the meeting together, they'd be locked, loaded, and ready to go in fifteen minutes. But if Richard was in the meeting, he'd slow things down. He'd ask too many questions. The consultant then added this: if they were honest with themselves, the outcome was better when Richard was in the room.

Mark told me the consultant's educated guess was exactly right. Mark realized that when Richard challenged people on everything, "He wasn't just being a pain in the butt," as he put it. Richard was adding something that nobody else could add. After that, Mark said, "We actually invited Richard to meetings where his subject matter expertise wasn't really the reason why we wanted him in the room. It was just the fact that we had too many people who were drivers in the room. We needed somebody like Richard who kind of pulled us back and said, 'Let's talk about emotions and people and all that kind of stuff.'"

They even started *intentionally* looking at people's personalities when they had meetings. They would ask the simple question, "Do we have somebody who gives us balance in the room?" If not, they would invite someone into the room who would slow them down, trip them up, and call them out.

Do you have somebody who brings balance to your room? Your life? Your thought processes? Only people with a healthy dose of humility and emotional intelligence can invite someone into the conversation who brings that balance.

This isn't easy. I saw a video on social media the other day that said we all need five people in our lives: a comforter, a confronter, a challenger, a counselor, and a celebrator.[63] Now, we all love hanging out with comforters and celebrators, and we typically appreciate good counselors (unless they tell us to do something we don't want to do... but that's another topic). But confronters and challengers? They're a whole lot of drama. So all too often, we shut down the conversations that should have been the richest and most productive because they also happen to be the cringiest and most painful.

It's hard to separate those things, though. If you're debating important, delicate, urgent matters, the conversation can't help but get a little intense, even a little emotional.

That's okay. It's a sign that people care.

You should be more scared of passionless meetings where everyone rubber-stamps your wonderful ideas and moves on to lunch. That's a sign of either disengagement or a lack of diversity. Don't mistake either of those for healthy collaboration.

Now, we could all probably name a few people who should probably try a little harder to get along. You know the kind. A few of them might be on your complicated persons list. Imagine, for example:

- **The arrogant loudmouths who think they are innately, infallibly qualified to have an opinion on everything.**

- **The chronic naysayers, or CAVE people: Citizens Against Virtually Everything.**

- **The combative types who play the devil's advocate way too often, maybe because they get a rush out of making people mad.**

- **The people with little emotional intelligence and zero filter who need to wise up and grow up.**

- **The individuals with a chip on their shoulder who were hurt in the past but, instead of dealing with it, just dump on everyone else.**

These people are out there, and they give conflict a bad name. But I think these people are in the minority. Most people need their job and wouldn't risk it lightly by randomly mouthing off. Most people are decent human beings and don't thrive on creating chaos. Most people have something to add to the conversation if they're given half a chance.

> **IF REASONABLY DECENT, INTELLIGENT INDIVIDUALS IN YOUR WORK CIRCLE ARE WILLING TO SPEAK UP, THEY DESERVE TO BE LISTENED TO AND RESPECTED.**

We all need a Richard. We all need someone who refuses to tell us only what we want to hear and is willing to disagree with us. How can you foster healthy disagreement? Let me share five suggestions:

I. FIGHT FAIR

The point of arguing or debating should always be to find the *solution* that is right and best, not to be the *person* who is right and best. A win is when healthy disagreement produces a robust, well-thought-out solution, a solution that was refined and forged by hard questions so it doesn't fall apart when faced with hard reality.

That means people can't fight dirty, including both you and the complicated individuals you deal with. This kind of group-powered, complex solution won't bubble to the surface if one or more of the voices in the room are willing to stoop to low blows just to get their way, stroke their ego, or stack their resume.

Dirty tactics include:

- **Bullying or intimidation**
- **Manipulation**
- **Threats or blackmail**
- **Guilt trips**
- **Gaslighting or other emotional abuse**
- **Character assassination**
- **Playing the victim**
- **Stonewalling or "silent treatment"**
- **Withholding information**
- **Lying or twisting the facts**

If you feel like someone is utilizing these tactics in a confrontation with you, you may want to have a sidebar conversation with them leveraging what I refer to in my previous book *Leveling Up* as intellectual humility. It's a great tool for confrontation because it helps you start conversations with, "I could be wrong."

"I could be wrong, but from what I heard you say and the vibe I got from it, it felt like you were intimidating or manipulating me into agreeing with you. But from what I know about you, that's probably not what you intended to communicate. Can you help me better understand what you're trying to communicate? What is your overall objective here?"

Don't put up with this kind of behavior, either in yourself or in others. It only empowers bullies and silences everyone else, which doesn't help anyone.

2. FIGHT FAST

Conflict *avoidance* is not a virtue. Conflict *management* is.

By *fight fast*, I mean don't let the conflict or disagreement brew for too long. There are times you need to sleep on it for a couple of days and allow yourself to get a different perspective, but I'd be cautious about waiting a couple of months. If you start sweeping things under the rug for months, years, or decades, you'll end up with a lot of built-up resentment. Then, because of the underlying resentment, every little thing feels bigger than life and feeds into a narrative of aggression.

How do you fight fast?

First, *get it out there*. Disagree as quickly as possible if you think something is dangerous or dumb. Speak up if there is a problem or an offense.

Sure, take some time to collect your thoughts and your data, but don't let that be an excuse to never speak up. It will only get harder if you wait longer.

People need to hear you. Make sure you express hard things in wise ways, but get it out there. Don't make disagreement a last resort. You're not speaking up out of selfishness, but out of courage. And you're not fighting for your way; you're contributing to finding the best way.

Second, *get it over with.* Don't drag the disagreement on forever. Speak your mind when it's time, honestly and even passionately. Then listen to other people do the same, and work it out.

I love watching sports teams duke it out on the court or the field, then shake hands and laugh together when the competition is over. It's obvious that many of the athletes respect and even like each other, despite the fact that they just tried to destroy each other during the game. Good athletes don't let off-the-court friendships interfere with their game, but they also don't let the game destroy their relationships.

Similarly, work disagreements should have a starting point and an ending point. Even if the result wasn't what you hoped for, once an agreement is reached or a decision is made, the fight is over. The bell rang. The whistle blew. Shake hands and move on.

3. FIGHT FACTUALLY

One CEO told me he lives by the mantra, "In God we trust. All others, bring data." He had experienced more than enough times how easy it is to get caught up in a clash of opinions, emotions, and ideas.

If you want to keep disagreements as objective as possible, stick to the facts. Not just your facts, and not just your interpretation of those facts, but all the facts. And since no single human knows everything, this means you listen to and learn from others in the room or on the call. You don't get bonus points for burying facts in order to bury your opponent.

We pick sides too easily, in my experience. We dig in our heels too quickly. We die on too many hills. It's unnecessary angst, though. In any disagreement, we need to keep our focus on which idea is *best*, not which idea is *ours*. In the long run, that will carry us further and cost us less.

If you really want to catch someone you're arguing with by surprise, when they state something you can agree with, say with all sincerity: "You're right. That's a good point. Tell me more."

They won't know what hit them.

Often, they'll lower their defenses so much they'll admit the weaknesses in their own argument or ask you what you think. One open-minded statement can change the whole mood. And even if the person doesn't open up in return, at least you've kept the focus on finding the truth, and you've gotten them to lay all their cards out on the table. That gives you an advantage.

There's another benefit here too. Other people will notice your commitment to truth over ego, and your street cred will rise. People will trust you more. You might not make progress with the complicated person who only wanted to speak their piece, but you just won points with everyone else by taking the high road.

When it comes to fighting factually, the goal is to get the best and broadest perspective you can. To help that happen, pay special attention to three kinds of people:

1. **THE VETERANS IN THE ROOM.** These are the people who bring the most lived experience to the table, either with the company or regarding the question at hand. They've heard it all and seen it all. Don't dismiss them as being "stuck in the past" or "out of touch." Nothing can replace their hands-on, hard-earned knowledge of the company, products, systems, processes, history, and market.

2. **THE NERDS IN THE ROOM.** By nerds, I mean those with training and technical understanding. They might not always be the most verbal, but they are often the most knowledgeable. Don't criticize them as being "too bogged down in the details." Details are their jam. They bring a perspective based on objective data and actual research, not simply gut feelings or past experiences.

3. **THE NEWBIES IN THE ROOM.** If someone has been on the staff, the board, or the project for only a few weeks or months, they have something everyone else has lost and can't get back: a fresh perspective. They see everything with new eyes, which means they'll notice issues others overlook and ask questions nobody else is curious about. They'll see blind spots, hidden opportunities, untapped markets, and novel applications. Make sure not to write them off as idealistic upstarts who are too young, too green, or too starry-eyed to have any good ideas.

These diverse perspectives are necessary, and all of them must work together. Each one is invaluable, but none of them is infallible. A wise leader or employee looks for ways to combine what everyone brings to the table to achieve better understanding and make smarter decisions.

4. FIGHT FOCUSED

As much as possible, conflict should focus on work-related issues, rather than letting personal feelings or personality clashes hijack the conversation. The Program on Negotiation at Harvard Law School identifies at least three categories of conflict:[64]

- **RELATIONAL CONFLICT** has to do with people. It refers to things like tension, friction, annoyance, frustration, and irritation. This is probably what you think of first when you hear the word *conflict*.

- **VALUE CONFLICT** has to do with fundamental differences in values and identity issues—things like politics, religion, ethics, and worldviews. I'm sure you can already see how tricky this one can be.

- **TASK CONFLICT** has to do with projects, processes, and goals. What should we do, and how should we do it? Of the three, this type of conflict has the most potential to move things forward.

In general, relational and value conflict should be kept to a minimum, while task conflict is often necessary and helpful—when you do it right.[65]

"To a minimum" is an important phrase because you are a human being. You don't unplug your emotions when you clock in to work. So if a task conflict is intense enough, it's probably going to feel at least a little bit relational. And because you definitely shouldn't disable your moral compass from nine to five, your values are going to be very present throughout the day too.

The goal here is awareness and focus. When you're butting heads with someone, ask yourself, *Is this conflict about our relationship? Is it about a difference in values? Or is it about the task?* Often the mere act of asking these questions will help you decide whether to minimize it or escalate it.

5. FIGHT FORWARD

The last suggestion for healthy disagreements is this: use conflict to move you forward. If two or more reasonably competent human beings don't see eye-to-eye on something, don't get mad; get interested. Both of you are good people. Smart people. Why assume one of you is wrong?

Maybe you're both right, and the conflict is pointing you toward the doorway into an entirely new solution. The disagreement is a gift. It's a clue. It's an opportunity to innovate. Instead of looking at differences as problems to be solved, treat them as stepping-off points for exploration.

In philosophy and logic, a "false dichotomy" refers to a scenario where you're given two options and told you must pick one of them when in reality there are other alternatives. It's binary thinking. It's an either/or mentality.

For example, the idea that you have to choose either family or career is a false dichotomy. I want both! So is the assumption you have to be either liberal or conservative (I'm somewhere in the middle), drink either coffee or tea (I'm team water), or like either cats or dogs (I despise them both).

There are always other options. You just have to look for them.

And the very act of looking will propel you forward.

We're too accustomed to approaching arguments as win-lose scenarios: either you win and I lose, or I win and you lose. But disagreement done right can be a win for everyone. Not a win in the sense that everyone gets exactly what they want, but in the sense that everyone's needs are taken into account, both as individuals and as a group.

Often the solution you land on when you're debating between two options is a third option. It might be a hybrid, or it might be an entirely new idea that no one could have come up with on their own, but everybody is at least sufficiently satisfied with it. It is the result of taking each other's concerns and needs seriously, then brainstorming and bouncing ideas off each other until the creative juices kick in.

Disagreement sparks creativity. Why? Because when you take seriously the needs of every person or department, you establish your constraints. Your nonnegotiables. And creativity is birthed out of constraint.

If the solution to the conflict was obvious, your competition would have found it already. Look at complicated conflict as a barrier to entry. Only the bravest, wisest, and most determined are able to push through the wall.

This principle applies to complicated requests too. Whether it's a raise, a time-off request, a deadline extension, a policy change, or anything else, don't allow yourself to become frustrated or hopeless when smart people push for hard things. I know it can feel like you're being asked to do the impossible, but maybe they have a point. Maybe there's a way for them to have what they need without you losing what you need. Look for a third option.

When there is disagreement, don't fall for the fallacy of a false dichotomy. Ask more questions. Do more research. Table the topic for a week so everyone can think about it some more. Keep looking until you find that elusive hybrid option that propels all of you forward together. Dealing with conflicts and disagreements is an art and a skill anyone can learn over time, regardless of their personality.

Here's a recap of these five ways to handle conflict and disagreement, since that was a lot of f-words to remember. (No, not *that* f-word.)

1. **FIGHT FAIR:** don't manipulate to get your way.

2. **FIGHT FAST:** get it out there and get it over with.

3. **FIGHT FACTUALLY:** stay objective and honest.

4. **FIGHT FOCUSED:** concentrate on the task at hand.

5. **FIGHT FORWARD:** come out stronger and smarter on the other side.

You can do this. Diversity, differences, and disagreements are an inevitable part of being members of the crazy, complex species we call humanity.

Don't deny it. Don't squash it.

Get better at it.

Sure, it's complicated. They are, and you are, and I am, and we are. But hidden in that complication is the strength that makes us great.

Now, I wish I could guarantee that the principles and practices we've explored throughout this book would take any working relationship, no matter how weird or wonky, from complicated to collaborative. It would be amazing to have a set of tools that would soften the hardest of hearts, open the narrowest of minds, and grease the squeakiest of connections.

If you've been in the workforce for any amount of time, though, you've likely come across at least one or two individuals who seem determined to thwart your best attempts at collaboration.

They've made "complicated" an art form, and they're proud of it.

These people are the reason for the subtitle of this book—strategies for effective collaboration with (nearly) anyone—and they are the reason you need to know how to set effective boundaries in the workplace. That is the topic we turn to next.

CHAPTER II

PUTTING THE "NEARLY" IN NEARLY ANYONE

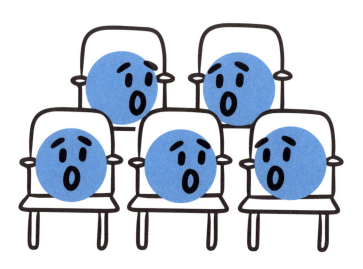

Sometimes when I'm speaking at an event, I'll say jokingly, "Every organization I've ever worked with had at least one person who should have been fired years ago, but because they are related to the boss, or they are friends with a major stakeholder, or they are golf buddies with a board member . . . here they are!"

I pause, then I say, "As a matter of fact, they might be sitting right next to you."

People always point at each other in mock horror.

But then I ask, more seriously, "So . . . what *are* they doing here?"

In that moment, some of the smartest people I know look dumbfounded. They remember times they had to come up with excuses to explain that person's presence in the workplace because they didn't want to go on record as being the person who said what everyone else is thinking: "No, they shouldn't be here."

Welcome to (nearly) anyone.

This is the chapter where we talk about your "nearly" person. Some people are just not capable of effective collaboration. They are the reason the subtitle of this book is what it is. They put the "nearly" in nearly anyone.

We've spent the last few chapters exploring ways to collaborate with complicated people. We've talked about proper expectations, self-awareness, empathy, a collaboration mindset, people skills, diverse generations, communicating with different levels of colleagues, and conflict and confrontation. But even with all that, you need to know something: you won't be able to effectively collaborate with *everyone.*

I wish that weren't the case, but it is. Some people won't do their part, no matter how hard you try to understand and connect with them.

BUT THAT'S NOT ON YOU; IT'S ON THEM.

For reasons known only to them and their therapist, they aren't just complicated to work with—they are impossible.

Now, I believe these impossibly complicated people are in the minority, and I also believe that some of them will change over time. But the fact remains that there are a few of them. Quite a few of them. Maybe there's a "nearly" near you. Maybe they are sitting two cubicles over, or one floor up, or on the other side of a Zoom call.

This is the individual who consistently (and maybe intentionally) tests the limits of your patience and the boundaries of workplace harmony. They could be the incessantly negative naysayer. They might be the office gossip who's spreading a "truth" that's actually false. Maybe they are the over-promiser and under-deliverer, or they are the narcissist who pressures everyone into supporting their mediocre ideas, or they are the inflexible know-it-all who refuses to accept that they might be wrong.

The ideal working relationship is when two sides come to the table with the belief that they both have room for improvement. But how do you collaborate with someone who refuses to meet you 10% of the way, much less halfway? How do you partner with someone who believes their toxic behavior is normal or justified and they don't need to change?

When you think about people like this, you might feel genuinely hopeless. You've tried, after all. You've given them feedback. You've gone to therapy. You've talked with HR. You've acknowledged your part. You've apologized for your mistakes. You even bought them a birthday card.

But nothing works, and nothing improves. They're unfireable, uncoachable, unchangeable, unapproachable, unfriendly, and unapologetic.

And that isn't going to change.

You have to make peace with the reality that you work with a "nearly" or two, so if quitting isn't in the cards for you, you're going to need to set some boundaries.

Boundaries are lines you draw that define what you will and will not allow in the workplace. They are limits you set and ground rules you follow. For example:

- **I don't answer emails or take calls when I'm on vacation.**

- **I only accept appointments on Mondays and Tuesdays.**

- **I don't hug coworkers of the opposite sex.**

- **I answer emails within a day.**

- **I refuse to gossip about coworkers or management.**

- **I won't allow other people's lack of planning to become my emergency.**

- **I can only handle requests that go through the proper channels.**

Did you find yourself saying, "Ha! That would be nice!" to any of those? That's exactly why boundaries are so hard. They can seem like wishful thinking.

Are they really, though? Or are we just afraid of the price we'd have to pay to set them?

To be fair, that price is real. If you play the "my way or the highway" card too often, you'll probably get the highway. On the other hand, if you never take the risk of pushing for what you need, you might spend eight hours a day in a toxic, unsafe environment.

BOUNDARIES ARE—
YOU GUESSED IT—
COMPLICATED.

But they are also crucial to collaborating with complicated people, especially the impossibly complicated ones who refuse to do their part.

Setting good boundaries is one of those ideas that sounds great on paper but is surprisingly hard to put into practice. It's one thing to tell yourself you won't stay at work an extra hour every day, but how do you tell your boss that, especially if seven other people would love to have your job and your boss is more than willing to pit you against each other for selfish gain?

In order to set better boundaries—i.e., ones that work—you need to understand what boundaries are *and* what they are meant to accomplish. Otherwise, you'll just make a wish list and then wonder why nothing changes.

Let's begin by looking at what boundaries are not capable of accomplishing.

WHAT BOUNDARIES CAN'T DO

If you expect boundaries to solve all your problems and simplify all your complicated people, you're heading down a short road toward big disappointment.

Boundaries are *not* designed to:

- **Control the other person's decisions**

- **Fix the other person's issues**

- **Make all your interactions easy**

- **Give you absolute control over your job experience**

- **Keep you aloof and separate from all the idiots out there**

- **Turn your workplace into Disneyland**

This is important because we tend to think of boundaries as a way to "deal with" complicated people. However, that makes boundaries about *them*, and boundaries are actually about *us*. They are a way for us to control what we can control, not a way to magically make challenging individuals meet our expectations.

The complicated person is still going to be complicated. They might even get more complicated for a while if they're no longer able to manipulate you, guilt you, or aggravate you.

That's their problem. That's their choice. You can't make them do anything . . . but they can't make you do anything either. Unless you let them.

Boundaries are a way to not let them.

The problem is, if you treat your boundaries as rules that other people have to follow, you're going to frustrate yourself to no end because some of those people are uncaring and uncontrollable. For example, if you expect a complicated colleague not to stop texting you about work issues after you leave for the day, you're putting the burden on them to stick to your boundary. While that's a reasonable request that a normal person would honor, a legitimately complicated person probably won't listen.

It's your boundary, though. Control what you can control. Instead of getting mad at their lack of etiquette, put your phone on Do Not Disturb. Someone will be annoyed. But you can politely say, "Hey, I put my phone on Do Not Disturb after seven in the evening because I really want my family to have my undivided attention." This makes the boundary about you and not about the other person's (annoying) behavior.

A general manager in the fitness industry told me that one of her assistant managers, whom I'll call Sarah, had a team member under her who told her outright that she didn't respect women in power. This woman wouldn't take direction from Sarah or listen to her in any way, just because of her gender.

That didn't just create a complicated working relationship; it also hurt Sarah's feelings, for obvious reasons. The GM had Sarah reach out to HR, and she also helped Sarah separate the job performance of this individual from her clearly toxic beliefs. The GM said, "It's not your job to judge how anybody feels or to get mad at somebody for the way that they see things. We're just here to manage people and how they do their jobs."

I think that's a great perspective in a complicated situation. Sarah couldn't control the team member's view of women in leadership, even though it was outright offensive. But she could focus on the work at hand and make sure the woman was doing her job.

While setting boundaries doesn't change anyone else, it does change you: how you respond, what you allow, how you feel, how you communicate, what consequences you enforce, and more. That is ultimately where your hope and autonomy can be restored.

Besides changing or controlling people, there is one more thing that boundaries can't do: they can't bring something back to life that needs to end.

There are certain relationships, projects, goals, and even jobs that might be beyond hope. At some point, you might need to cut your losses and simply move on. This is a book about collaboration, after all, not martyrdom.

In his book *Necessary Endings,* Dr. Henry Cloud writes, "Endings are not only part of life; they are a requirement for living and thriving, professionally and personally. Being alive requires that we sometimes kill off things in which we were once invested, uproot what we previously nurtured, and tear down what we built for an earlier time."[66]

Ending something important is hard, and it should be hard. If it's easy for you to terminate relationships or goals or jobs, you might not have been very invested in the first place.

The process of ending an important relationship or work commitment is not one to be taken lightly. You know this. But when you know it's time, move with confidence. Don't keep setting boundaries that will be violated, making rules that will be broken, trying strategies that won't work, and begging impossibly complicated people to behave.

END THINGS WELL SO YOU CAN STEP INTO A BETTER FUTURE.

WHAT BOUNDARIES CAN DO

If boundaries aren't about changing or controlling people, what are they meant to accomplish? Let me give you three things boundaries will do for you:

I. BOUNDARIES KEEP YOU SAFE

A truly complicated person, the "nearly" in nearly anyone, is a threat. They threaten your job performance; your emotional, mental, or physical health; the unity of the team; the workplace environment; and the success of the company.

One of the goals of boundaries, then, is to minimize that threat. For example, maybe someone makes you uncomfortable because they insist on hugging people, giving back rubs, and things like that. They call it being affectionate or friendly, but you feel like it crosses a line. You can set a boundary: "The only physical touch I allow at work is shaking hands." And along with that, you can set a consequence: "If you violate that physical boundary, I will report it to HR."

Is that intense? Is that being "too sensitive" or "hard to work with"? No, it's reasonable, and it's right, and it needs to happen. And it's a whole lot better than letting the discomfort continue, avoiding being in the same room with the person, or feeling genuinely threatened if you are in an elevator together or work late on the same evening.

Your boundaries are your choice. You have to determine what you need in order to work safely and effectively. Someone else might draw different lines, and that's fine, as long as you both respect each other's boundaries.

Exactly what constitutes "safe" is something to evaluate carefully. Safe can't mean "free from all discomfort and pain," because life is full of discomfort and pain, and often what you want the most is hidden on the other side of that rough road. David Goggins is a former Marine and Navy SEAL who has run over sixty ultra-distance races. In his autobiography *Can't Hurt Me*, he reflects on all the hardships he endured to become successful, then says this: "I was the sum total of the obstacles I'd overcome."[67]

I love that. Pushing through a certain amount of pain and difficulty has a way of shaping you and forging you into the person you are capable of being.

Although in some situations pain should be pushed through and overcome, in other situations it needs to be listened to because it's trying to tell you something important. I've seen leaders and friends who seemed incredibly strong and resilient on the outside ultimately spiral into anxiety disorders because they pushed themselves too hard for too long. In the name of doing more or being more, they didn't listen to their body's signals to slow down or set different boundaries.

Try to find that sweet spot where you can avoid genuine harm but still weather your share of storms.

2. BOUNDARIES MAKE YOU MORE PRODUCTIVE

While boundaries protect your safety as a person, they also protect your productivity as a worker. Setting boundaries at work should ultimately improve your job performance and environment. How?

- **You can have a healthier work-life balance, which allows you to show up at work rested and recharged. You'll be less grouchy and more energetic.**

- **You don't have to waste so much emotional energy during the day on unhealthy interactions or impossible demands.**

- **You can focus on your own work without being distracted by tasks you aren't supposed to be doing or fixing.**

- **You can move out of defense mode and into creative mode.**

- **Your example can motivate others to maintain healthy boundaries, which improves the work environment for everyone.**

Boundaries are for you, but they also serve the greater interest of the team. Don't look at them as selfish demands but rather as a way to bring your best self to work every day. This mentality gives you perspective on what boundaries are reasonable, and it also gives you leverage to insist on the boundaries you really need.

If there is truly an emergency that requires all hands on deck, you might need to set aside some boundaries for a bit. We've all had to "take one for the team" at times. The success of the team is probably what pays your salary, so don't resent putting in a little extra from time to time. That's what teamwork is all about. But if "emergencies" are happening multiple times a week, that's another story. Often, it's these repeated violations of your boundaries that indicate you're dealing with an impossibly complicated person. Don't let yourself be manipulated into making exceptions time after time.

There's a time factor involved here, of course. You might not get all your preferences, at least right off the bat, so have realistic expectations, focus on making forward progress over time, and choose which boundaries are "hard" (nonnegotiables you won't budge on) and which are "soft" (preferences you could adjust).[68] In a sense, you're creating a personal work culture within a larger office or company culture. It takes time to reset people's expectations about how available you are, what meetings you go to, how quickly you respond to emails, whose problems you solve, or what tasks you're willing or able to do. Be patient with people and yourself, but keep making progress.

And remember, boundaries are always going to be a little messy. That's okay. The world around you is always shifting and changing, which means you have to shift and change your expectations and habits as well. You can't expect to carve your Ten Boundaries into stone tablets like some modern-day Moses and never think about them again.

This is especially true when a fresh batch of complicated people cycles into your workplace. Don't be surprised if/when you have to spend some time both rethinking and recommunicating your boundaries. It's part of life, and it will happen.

3. BOUNDARIES KEEP YOU CONNECTED

This last one is incredibly important, and I don't think it gets enough airtime. Oftentimes, when it comes to boundaries, we focus mostly on the previous points about safety and productivity. The problem is, that can lead to a very defensive, isolated, siloed posture.

Humans aren't meant to live like that.

We aren't meant to work like that either.

The magic happens in the connections, after all. In the interactions, in the differences, in the complexity.

Even if you work with a really, really complicated person, you still have to *work with* them. Boundaries don't take that reality away; they just set ground rules to help you work with that person with minimal damage and maximum effectiveness.

Boundaries are about you filling in this blank: "If I'm going to work with you, then I need _____." You're communicating your intention to collaborate along with the conditions that will make that collaboration possible. Your boundaries are simply a means to an end: working together as safely and effectively as possible.

Obviously, you won't enjoy the same level of effective collaboration that you would have if they'd gotten their act together a little. You might have to minimize contact. You might need to keep things formal and strictly business. It might be more of a truce between enemies (or frenemies) than an agreement to be allies, but at least you can set ground rules that enable ongoing interaction. It's not ideal, but it is tolerable.

This is where boundaries really take on power. If you don't like each other or see eye to eye on pretty much anything, you can still use boundaries to define your connections, and connections lead to collaboration. Your boundaries are where you connect. They are what unites you, not what separates you.

A boundary is not meant to be a heavily guarded castle wall surrounded by a moat filled with hungry crocodiles. It's more like a picket fence. Here's how you can visualize the difference between those two dividers:

- **A castle wall is DEFENSIVE: it's focused on keeping people out who probably have evil intentions.**

- **A picket fence is DELINEATIVE: it marks the line between two people's property, but it still allows for connection and conversation.**

You can chat across a picket fence. You can keep an eye on each other's property and help each other watch out for danger. You can lend each other tools or give each other cookies. Each of you are chilling in your own backyards, but those yards are adjacent, so you're always connected.

The problem with impossibly complicated people is that they often don't understand where their backyard ends and yours begins. They encroach on your territory and override your autonomy. They make unreasonable demands. They have ridiculous expectations. They hijack your time, energy, and skills to meet their needs because their needs are all that matter to them.

Boundaries draw that line for them since they are incapable of drawing it themselves. It's your way of reminding them in practical, tangible ways, "This is where your influence over me ends and my autonomy begins."

My concern with boundaries that are too defense-focused is that they can get in the way of the collaboration we need. In an interview with a C-suite executive in the retail industry, I asked if she thought someone could be an effective collaborator without bringing something personal to the table. She said that in her opinion, you can't. There has to be something connecting you, some sort of connection that people can sense and feel. She told me you have to let people in to at least a point.

Healthy boundaries are about letting people into your world without letting them run your world. Better boundaries equal better connections. And better connections equal greater collaboration.

Is that easy? Of course not. Is it possible? I think so. At least in most cases. If not, if the person you work with is genuinely harming you and you've already exhausted every avenue available, you might need to quit. As I said earlier, life is too short and you're too valuable to sell your soul to a toxic work environment.

But don't start with the assumption that an impossibly complicated person means an impossible work environment. Assume the opposite: if you can create and communicate the right set of boundaries, you might figure out a way to make this working relationship actually work.

HOW TO SET EFFECTIVE BOUNDARIES

We've spent the last few pages talking about the importance and benefits of setting boundaries, both to you and those you work with. Ultimately, though, you have to decide what boundaries to set and when to set them.

What is most important to you? What is most urgent? What are the nonnegotiables? What are reasonable asks? When and how should you implement them? What would have to change in order for this to happen?

These are questions only you can answer. You might have to wrestle with them for a while, but that wrestling is leading to progress. It's a much better use of your mental and emotional energy than stewing and stressing over the stupid things your complicated person did that day.

Here are a few practical ways to get started in setting effective boundaries:

I. START WITH SMALL BOUNDARIES AND QUICK WINS

Have you ever walked around for two hours with a pebble in your shoe because you were too busy to take it out? It's amazing the amount of irritation something so small can cause, and it's equally amazing how quickly we could solve some things if we took the time to do it.

If you're feeling overwhelmed, exhausted, or borderline hopeless because a complicated person seems intent on ruining your life, think of some small things you could easily implement. These are quick wins or easy fixes that will at least lower the temperature a little.

In a sense, they are hacks. They are cheat codes to reclaim at least a portion of your autonomy and sanity. For example:

- Use headphones and/or close your door to avoid interruptions.
- Turn off phone notifications when you need to focus.
- Set out-of-office replies when you don't want to be reachable.
- Schedule breaks or focused work time into your calendar rather than letting it fill up until you're swamped.
- Have a "no borrowing" policy for items you use regularly.
- Set clear meeting expectations (topics and time limit) in advance.
- Set hard stops for phone calls.
- Shake hands rather than hugging people, if physical boundaries are needed.
- Leave work at work rather than taking your laptop or work phone home every day.
- Answer emails and texts on your timetable (within reason, of course), not theirs.
- Say, "I'll add that to my to-do list" rather than dropping everything to attend to the need.

What pebbles are bothering you the most that might be the easiest to fix? What things are complicated people doing that drive you crazy? What things are even relatively *uncomplicated* people doing that make your life even more complicated? What are the pain points and the pressure points?

Once you've identified some of these, ask yourself: *What could I do differently right now that would relieve some of the stress, pressure, or frustration I feel?* You might be surprised how obvious some of the solutions are once you decide to do what you can do instead of feeling hopeless about what you cannot.

2. PRACTICE THE ART OF SAYING NO

Setting boundaries doesn't have to result in hurt feelings or a cold war. With effort and care, you can usually do it in a kind, wise way that maximizes results and minimizes negative repercussions.

Saying no is one of my least favorite things to do. Unfortunately, the nature of my work means I have to turn down more invitations to speak than I can accept. I hate it. It's never easy to disappoint someone. I spend a surprising amount of time finding ways to decline things without harming a relationship or causing unnecessary awkwardness.

Whatever your line of work might be, I'm sure you've experienced similar pressures. You're expected to attend twenty hours of weekly meetings and still get forty hours of work done. You're pressured to accept yet another project when you're already overworked and underpaid. You are subtly shamed if you don't keep up with emails even on the weekend.

Don't say yes to everything, but don't say no in a way that might cost you your job. Spend some time thinking about your reply so it comes across in the most gracious but firm way possible.

Let's say your complicated boss gets angry that you didn't reply to their email at eight p.m. last night. Rather than saying, "Sorry, you don't pay me enough for that," you could say, "You know, my kids are young, and bedtime is really important for us in this season, so I generally don't check my email after I leave work. But I'll always get back to you first thing in the morning."

Or maybe a procrastinating coworker begs you to help them finish a project at the last minute. Instead of snapping, "That was your job, and your irresponsibility doesn't constitute my emergency," you could say, "Unfortunately, I have some things I can't move in my schedule, so I'm not going to be able to help you with this today. But is there something I could do later this week?"

Notice that, in these examples, you're saying no more often, you're saying it with grace, and you're keeping the focus on what you can do rather than on what they should or shouldn't do. You don't have to solve their problems, although you should try to be empathetic toward them. Ultimately, though, it's your responsibility to set your boundaries, and it's theirs to figure out how to get their job done without violating them.

3. IT'S NOT A BOUNDARY UNTIL IT'S COMMUNICATED

It's not enough to tell yourself what you will and won't stand for; you have to make others aware of it. You can't get mad at someone for overstepping boundaries they didn't know existed. Maybe they have no problem whatsoever with taking working vacations, and since you always write them back on your vacations, they assume you're cool with it too. That's on you, not them. You have to draw the line or they'll draw one for you.

Remember, too, that actions speak louder than words, so if you don't respect your own boundaries by the way you act and react, other people won't either. When you say you won't do something and then you do it anyway, you're sending mixed messages, and they're going to believe the message that benefits them the most.

This isn't a one-time thing. Many times, we are victims of what could be called "boundary creep." We draw a line, but that line gets worn down or moved, one exception at a time. Psychologist Dr. Rebecca Ray states, "Boundary creep is when someone tests the limits of a boundary using their relationship with you as grounds to sneak across the line in ways that seem perfectly acceptable to the naked eye."[69]

They might say things like:

- **"Can you do this, just this once?"**

- **"Would you do it for me?"**

- **"I know you understand how important this is."**

- **"I'm sure I can rely on you."**

- **"You've never let me down."**

Do any of these things sound familiar?

Now, as I said before, you can make exceptions to your own boundaries. Just be aware that every exception weakens that boundary—and for really complicated people, one exception might be all it takes for them to discard your rule completely. They are probably used to getting their way through manipulative tactics like this.

If your boundary is good, reasonable, and well communicated, you generally should feel no obligation to give in to their tactics. It's your boundary, not theirs. And since it's there for the good of your working relationship, it's to their benefit to respect it too.

4. KEEP IT CLASSY

Don't fight toxicity with toxicity, and don't fight complicated with more complicated. Just because someone else is behaving in a certain way doesn't mean you have to. As I said in the last chapter, make sure you're staying true to your values and character.

One of the main things to watch out for when setting boundaries with complicated people is your words. When you're drawing lines and laying down the law, emotions are probably going to be all over the place. You should do your best to maintain equilibrium, but you're going to feel all the feels. That doesn't mean you have to say all the words, though. Instead, you might:

- **Wait a day before sending that angry email. Then reread it and take out some of the nasty bits. Alternately, use an AI writing tool to reword your hot-tempered first draft into something that is firm but still professional. Your emotions will die down, but emails are forever, my friend.**

- **Tell a belligerent colleague, "Let me think about that for a while," rather than telling them exactly what you think about it right now. You are a human, not an android, and your tone and body language are going to say a lot of things you don't want to say if you confront the person right now.**

- **Use language that is professional and courteous, even if the person is the opposite of that. You are still a professional. You don't have to stoop to their tactics or let their behavior dictate yours.**

One of the problems with boundaries is that we often wait too long to set them, so when we finally do, there's a lot of pent-up frustration and hurt involved. That can come across as defensive and retaliatory. Remember to keep it classy. Even if they're getting on your last nerve, it's possible to defend and protect yourself in a professional way.

5. EMBRACE THE POWER OF DOCUMENTATION

Keep a record. Documenting instances of unprofessional or disruptive behavior can be invaluable, especially when discussions with management or HR become necessary. Don't view it as plotting a case against someone, but rather as having a clear, objective way to explain how their behavior impacts the team's performance and your ability to collaborate effectively.

Part of the challenge of workplace conflicts is that they are often feelings-based, and both parties see them or remember them differently. If you can provide documentation to back up your boundary, you might be able to help complicated people (and their supervisors or other authorities) see why the boundary is necessary. Even if they don't agree with it, they will at least have specific examples of what behavior needs to change.

If you've ever set any boundaries (and I'm sure you have, even if you didn't call them that), you can probably add to this list. It's an art, as I mentioned, which means it's something you can practice, improve, and learn.

I hate to say it, but setting boundaries is a skill you'll need as long as you work with people. All you have to do is Google "books about boundaries" or "books about confrontation" to realize that this issue is not new, and it's not going away. Some of the book titles are great too: *Collaborating with the Enemy . . . How to Hug a Porcupine . . . Surrounded by Idiots*. Just the titles make me feel seen.

Boundaries won't solve all your problems at work, but they'll help. They'll move you forward a little. They'll give you back some of your autonomy and restore some of your hope. They'll set ground rules for effective collaboration, or they'll make it clear when something needs to come to an end.

Don't let the "nearly" in nearly anyone become the nemesis who haunts your nightmares or the reason you quit your job. Set healthy boundaries, demand respect, and keep collaborating. You are always in charge of you.

CHAPTER 12

      A   B   C

1.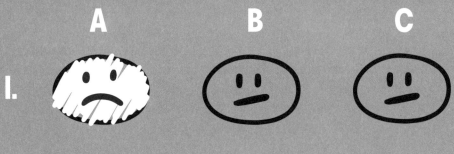

2.

3.

4.

CHOICES THAT CHANGE YOU, EVEN IF PEOPLE STAY THE SAME

When I'm booked to speak to an organization, I work with them in advance to figure out the content that will best serve their people. I usually ask about their pain points and the challenges their employees and leaders are facing.

I'll never forget getting ready to speak to a group of nine hundred leaders of a large airline. I met with their leadership team several weeks before my talk about how I could best serve them, and one of their executives asked me to share on a subject no corporate or C-suite leader had ever requested.

FORGIVENESS.

Now, I don't have a problem talking on forgiveness. I actually got my start as a professional speaker by speaking in churches. In that setting, I knew the people listening to me lived out their faith at work every day, so when I spoke, I would often use work-related examples. Eventually, business leaders in those audiences started to say, "Ryan, why don't you come do this talk at my company? If everybody at my workplace acted how you just described, I think it would change everything. We'd have better morale, better customer service, and better sales." One thing led to another, and now I spend a lot of time in both worlds: corporate and church.

Here's what's interesting about the church space: forgiveness is a conversation that happens every weekend. Why? Because forgiveness is a lot easier when you believe that it's been given to you first. As a person of faith, I believe God sent his Son to die in place of humanity, and because of that, I have experienced forgiveness, peace, and acceptance. Every weekend church service is a natural moment to reflect on God's forgiveness toward us, which then translates into extending forgiveness to others.

That's the church world, though. That's the faith space. This airline exec and the others on the call represented corporate America. How could I talk about forgiveness to a bunch of leaders in a Fortune 100 company without getting overly religious? What would that mean?

We kept talking. The executive told me that forgiveness was one of their biggest needs. He said, "We have so many people here that are holding on to bitterness. It's like they're picking at a twenty-year-old scab, expecting it to heal." That metaphor, graphic as it was, stuck with me. He was right. Sometimes there's a colleague who bad-mouthed you to your boss, took the credit for your idea or work, blamed you for something that wasn't your fault, stole a client or commission, sabotaged a project you were working on, harassed or insulted you, or even got you fired.

How often do we hang on to past offenses and grudges, rolling them over in our minds, replaying conversations and reliving betrayals, all the while thinking that somehow we're helping ourselves heal?

Anyone who has been in the workplace for any amount of time probably has personal horror stories for several of those scenarios, plus a few more. The reality is the minute you go to work, you are susceptible to a certain amount of offense and relational pain.

> **In our survey, 59% of people reported experiencing anger or bitterness in the last year due to working with complicated people. That's a painfully high number. Earlier, I shared some of the findings related to mental health—including people who have had suicidal thoughts—that are highly concerning. Complicated people aren't just making work less efficient; they are also causing pain that digs deep into our hearts and minds and creates open wounds.**

What do you do with that hurt?

Do you hide it? Deny it? Bury it? Feed it? Resent it? Numb it? Lose yourself in it?

Or do you acknowledge it, process it, and find a way forward?

We talked about boundaries earlier, so you already know forgiveness can't mean leaving yourself in a place of ongoing harm. Go ahead and set boundaries. Practice all the other things we've discussed so far. But if you stop short of forgiveness, you're probably going to struggle to find peace and healing.

That might seem unfair. *Why should I forgive them?* you might wonder. *They don't deserve it. They're not going to change. They need to change, not me.*

Here's the thing: forgiveness is for you, not them.

It's about your freedom, not theirs.

It's about making things right within you even when wrong has been done to you.

Forgiveness is a little like decluttering your desk. Suddenly, there's more space to think, create, and collaborate. What a lot of people don't realize about grudges is that they require a constant investment of energy, and it's energy they could be using to get work done.

I get that sometimes people do things that feel unforgivable, but what's your endgame with that strategy? Avoid them for the rest of your career? Hate them forever? Carry that hurt into new relationships and jobs? That's what the airline executive was talking about when he mentioned twenty-year-old wounds that had never healed.

I love how James Clear puts it:

> **HOLDING ON TO ANGER** and resentment is like scuba diving with an anchor. As long as you're clinging to it, you're bound to the seabed, limited in movement, unable to appreciate the coral reefs and the colorful fish that dart in and out of view.
>
> **Forgiveness is letting go** of the anchor. It isn't about declaring what was done to you is okay, but about unburdening yourself so you can swim freely. Forgiveness is a gift you give yourself. It's the gift of letting go of the anchors you've been carrying.[70]

If forgiveness is possible—and I think it is—it changes the game for you, and it changes the game for your company.

So how on earth do you do that? How do you let go of the anchor holding you captive and swim into the waters of freedom?

By making a few choices.

I. CHOOSE THE KIND OF COLLEAGUE YOU WANT TO BE

Have you ever had a colleague who would say things like, "No offense, but . . . " and then proceed to offend you? It's like they thought the disclaimer gave them diplomatic immunity from the standards of human decency or social etiquette.

There are a few other phrases that are often used the same way. Maybe you've been the recipient of some of these:

- "It's none of my business . . ." (sticks their nose directly in your business)

- "I probably shouldn't say this . . ." (says it anyway)

- "I don't mean to criticize . . ." (proceeds to drop an absolute bomb)

- "Not to sound rude . . ." (makes the rudest comment ever)

- "Don't take this the wrong way . . ." (says something that can't possibly be taken the right way)

- "I hate to tell you this . . ." (tells you something with obvious enjoyment)

- "I don't want to step on anyone's toes . . ." (stomps on literally everyone's toes)

Then the person walks away and continues on with their day, while you find yourself blown to bits by an uninvited truth bomb (that may or may not actually be true). Sometimes their careless, callous comments live rent-free in your head for days or months or years to come.

People like this tend to get a reputation for being rude, offensive, and mean. That's the kind of coworker they've decided to be. Maybe they didn't consciously choose it, but they're not choosing something else, so by default, they've become the complicated person everyone else has to watch out for.

The good news is that you get to choose for yourself how you want to show up at work. You don't have to let the snarkiness or the sarcasm of the office shape you. You don't have to let the gossip or the cliques control you. Regardless of your personality, upbringing, belief system, or work environment, you can choose what kind of colleague you're going to be to others. You can't change yesterday, but you can make choices today that transform your tomorrow.

One of the choices that will most define you in the workplace is something many people tend to overlook: the choice to be a forgiving person. You don't stumble into letting go of grudges; you choose your way into it. Along the way, you choose what kind of person you're going to be.

The hardest part about forgiveness is deciding you want to embrace it. Most people prefer to hold on to their anger, but you'd be surprised what can happen when you say out loud, "I want to be a forgiving person."

Researchers who have looked at conflict in the workplace have found compelling evidence that, over time, forgiveness leads directly to better work outcomes, including higher job satisfaction, higher work engagement, and lower burnout rates.[71] Remember, you don't need to forgive people just for their sake; forgiveness is for your sake. It's part of keeping yourself healed, healthy, and protected.

You don't *have* to be a forgiving person, by the way. Nobody is forcing you to choose this path. But you need to know it's possible. It's not out of reach. This doesn't mean becoming a doormat, but rather opening the door to becoming something different.

No offense, and it's none of my business, and I probably shouldn't say this, and I don't mean to criticize, and don't take this the wrong way, and I don't want to step on anyone's toes . . . but if your default is bitterness, you're not helping your future self.

You're one decision away from changing everything, though.

What kind of colleague do you want to be?

2. CHOOSE TO LET GO OF THE SMALL STUFF

Let's be real: the office is a petri dish for petty grudges. From battles over the thermostat to wars waged over the last donut, the opportunities to get peeved are endless. And let's not forget about email etiquette—or the lack thereof. Nothing brews a grudge faster than a passive-aggressive email cc'ing the whole department.

If you think about what exactly puts you off and ticks you off about your colleagues, you'll probably notice something: some of these things feel bigger than they actually are. I would even go as far as to say most of them probably are that way.

Unlike my speaking engagements, which involve talking to a lot of people, my coaching practice is about listening to a few people. In my years of inviting people to tell me about the urgent, pressing people problems that are occupying their headspace, I've watched countless clients have an epiphany in real time. As they describe out loud to me—a neutral outsider—the failures, betrayals, conflicts, or aggressions they feel are so huge, they often stop and say, "This whole thing started small, but it kinda blew up . . . I guess I'm making it a bigger deal than it should be."

We've all been there. Petty grievances have a way of taking on lives of their own if they aren't dealt with quickly, sometimes even developing into full-on office feuds. I read a story about someone who was tired of a coworker talking loudly on his desk phone all the time, so he came in early one day, unscrewed the phone mouthpiece, and hid a piece of salami with mustard inside it. Over the next couple of days, it started to stink, and the guy couldn't figure out what smelled so bad.

Another person was so strapped for cash that all they took to work for lunch one day was a jar of applesauce. Somebody stole it out of the fridge, ate it all, and left the empty jar on the counter. So the owner of the applesauce opened the refrigerator and threw out everybody's food, yelling, "If I can't eat, nobody is going to eat!" (Luckily, in that case, HR stepped in and bought pizza for everyone.)

They might make for tragically funny stories, but petty acts of revenge aren't exactly a sustainable solution or a healthy one, and they keep you fixated on issues that don't deserve your time and energy. That only makes your suffering worse, not better. One researcher who studied revenge summarized his findings this way: "One of the things that avengers do unintentionally is to prolong the unpleasant encounter. Those who don't have a chance to take revenge are forced, in a sense, to move on and focus on something different. And they feel happier."[72]

So how do we deal with petty offenses and grudges? First, acknowledge them for what they are: small potatoes. In the grand scheme of things, is it really worth losing sleep over the fact that someone stole your coffee mug? Probably not. Instead of plotting your revenge by hiding their mouse (tempting as that may be), try laughing it off . . . even if it's more of the "I'm laughing so I don't scream" kind of laugh.

Second, choose to let go. The beauty of letting go of petty grudges is that it leaves room for more important things, like enjoying your work or putting yourself in a better position to get that promotion. Plus, when you stop sweating the small stuff, you become Teflon to the office drama. Insults? Misunderstandings? They slide right off. Suddenly, you're not just enduring your job; you're flourishing in it, all because you chose not to let the little things hold you hostage.

Letting go of the small stuff doesn't make complicated people right. But it does set you free.

Sometimes we hang on to things for too long. We take things too personally. We remember insults we should forget. We internalize stuff we should shake off. We believe criticisms from people who don't even know us and whose opinions don't matter.

WE WASTE TIME
AND ENERGY
STEWING
AND STRESSING
OVER THE PAST
INSTEAD OF
MOVING FORWARD
IN HOPE.

We grow smaller instead of larger, harder instead of softer, bitter instead of better.

Besides our freedom, there's another benefit to quickly and easily letting go of the small stuff: we can often find something positive hidden within the complicated. Maybe it's a truth we needed to hear. Maybe it's better understanding of the other person. Maybe it's growth in our character or our career. But if we're overly focused on the mess that is the messenger, we can miss the gift within the encounter.

This isn't easy. When someone criticizes or contradicts us, it feels rather good to say, "They don't know what they're talking about. They have something against me. They don't see the whole picture. That's just the kind of person they are. What an idiot. What a jerk."

Unfortunately, even jerks can have a good point. Even idiots can tell you something you need to hear.

If you reject something that's true just because you don't like the person delivering it, that's like refusing to accept an Amazon package because the delivery guy was rude to you. What matters most is what's inside the box, not how it arrives. When you feel upset or hurt, take a minute to evaluate this question: "What is the gift I'm being given inside this complicated package?"

You don't have to like them or even respect them in order to receive from them. Maybe 80% of the interaction is nonsense. Choose to ignore the nonsense, but hang on to the 20% that's useful. It's a gift.

I'm convinced that learning to let go of the small stuff prepares us to let go of the big stuff. This is where forgiveness gets tricky, but it's also where it gets powerful. Maybe you were betrayed by a partner, or a coworker got you fired unjustly, or another salesperson stole your biggest account, or your company cut your position after twenty years of faithful service. Things like that hurt like crazy, but they're not the end of your story.

Honestly, much of the growth I've experienced in life has come in part as the result of pain. That's just how we are as humans. Sometimes life has to kick us in the butt before we'll get moving. Unfortunately, life often uses complicated people to do the kicking.

What they did should not have happened. But it did, and even though it hurt you, it also shaped you, and you came out stronger on the other side.

Choose to let go of the small stuff (and even the not-so-small stuff). It's not worth your time, your energy, or your strength. There are too many good things waiting for you out there.

3. CHOOSE TO GIVE BITTERNESS AN EXPIRATION DATE

Hurt happens. Offenses take place. People are complicated, and they say dumb stuff and do dumb stuff. They ghost you. They lie about you. They give you a look that makes you feel some type of way. They make a culturally insensitive remark.

Sometimes these things are accidental, and sometimes they are intentional. You can't really do anything about whether or not they happen, but you can make a plan for when they happen.

Here's a plan: be hurt, but don't stay hurt.

When something bad goes down, start by acknowledging the damage it did and the pain you feel. You don't get extra credit or a cash bonus for gaslighting yourself into thinking you're totally fine if you're not, or into believing nothing happened when it did. If you're mad about what someone did or said, that's okay. Be mad for a while. Be bitter for a bit.

I think this is especially important if you don't have the chance to confront them or have a conversation with them. You might need to spend some time processing the pain. There's no shame in that.

Have you ever been talking with a friend about how deeply someone else hurt you, and the friend interrupts mid-sentence to say: "You know, you just have to let it go." *Just let it go? As if it were that easy. And who are you to tell me that? You aren't the victim here.* Sometimes you get the feeling people want you to forgive and forget because *your* pain is making *them* uncomfortable.

Forgiveness has to be different than that and deeper than that. It has to be a choice you make by yourself and for yourself, not because you were forced into it.

You don't have to forget what was done or pretend it wasn't a terrible thing. But you can objectively criticize someone's offensive behavior while simultaneously choosing not to hold it against them until the day you die. You can unplug the emotional desire to make them pay. After all, it's exhausting to hate people like that. And when you hold something against someone forever, you're not giving them a life sentence. You're giving yourself one.

Do you really need to keep score all the time? Is that helping you? The more tally marks you add to that internal hurt list, the more weight and hate you're stuck pulling behind you. I don't think anyone on their deathbed wishes they had held more grudges, made more enemies, or hated more people. That kind of inner angst will chew you up and leave you with nothing to show for it.

So yes, let yourself feel all the feels. But don't stay there forever. Don't become a chronically mad person, a hurt person, or a bitter person. I've seen too many people move into an anger neighborhood toward their colleagues and never move out.

Here's a strategy you can use. Imagine whatever it was that the person did, from the petty to the egregious. Go back to the scene of the crime, look at the offense objectively, and ask yourself, *How long do I want this to affect me?*

It's a simple question but a serious one. What's your plan here? What's your endgame? What timeline are you going to put on this thing before you stop mourning it and stop hating them?

I don't think any human on the planet would watch an offense happen and say, "You know, I'd just love for this to impact me for the next two decades." And yet, there are people doing exactly that.

Now, I understand there can be deep, lasting trauma associated with harmful behavior. Most of us, maybe all of us, have experienced painful things that will stay with us forever and have even helped shape who we are. While we can't just decide not to feel those things, we can decide not to become bitter people.

So give your grudge an eviction notice. Pick a date on the calendar when you want to be over this thing. Maybe give yourself six months to let out your frustrations. When that date arrives, the past won't change, but your future will. You're giving yourself permission to move on.

If that takes work, put in the work. If it takes therapy, go to therapy. If it requires some hard conversations, get them on the calendar. Your goal is to take active steps toward putting these things behind you, to the best of your ability, so you can set your future self free.

4. CHOOSE TO FORGIVE COWORKERS BEFORE THEY HURT YOU

I was recently at an event with talk show host and author Dr. Phil. He mentioned that we make two kinds of decisions. Some are small, such as what we're going to eat or wear, while others are "life decisions" about our values and behavior. Life decisions are choices we make once and then never have to revisit. For example, Dr. Phil decided a long time ago that in business dealings, he will always "out-fair" the other person. In other words, he decided that in negotiations he always wanted the other side to have the better end of the stick. That way he never has to cross to the other side of the street when he sees someone coming. Instead, he'll know he treated them with generosity. He doesn't have to evaluate how he's going to behave each time he's in negotiations because that life choice guides him.

When I heard him speak, my mind instantly went to a life decision I made a long time ago: *I choose to forgive people before they hurt me.* If someone insults me, betrays me, talks about me behind my back, or does anything else that hurts me, I don't have to decide every time if I'm going to forgive them or not. Of course their meanness will sting, but I'm not going to let moments of hurt turn into months or even years of bitterness. I'm going to forgive them.

I call this pre-forgiveness. Pre-forgiveness is deciding I'm going to forgive people who haven't even hurt me yet. Today, somebody on my team might get an attitude with me because they've got stuff going on that I can't see. Somebody might cut in front of me in the security line at the airport. Somebody might cancel a speaking engagement.

So, I choose in advance to let that go. I decide to be predisposed to forgiveness. I'm anticipating their humanity this week and hoping they'll make space for mine.

Remember, if you're going to work with people (robots are a possibility, but they're complicated too), flawed ones are your only option. I wish it weren't that way. Maybe if we were more like ants or bees or birds, we'd move together in perfect harmony, building beautiful things and never hurting each other's feelings. Of course, we'd also be way down on the food chain, and that has some real disadvantages. I prefer to be human. In the grand scheme of life, apex predator status is even better than platinum airline miles status.

Maybe you didn't know that pre-forgiveness was an option, but it is. You have to choose it, though. This is about deciding in advance who you're going to be, how you're going to show up when tensions run high, and what you're capable of doing.

In other words, since you can't plan your way around complicated people, plan your way into forgiveness. Do you see the difference? Some people go to work like Eeyore, expecting the worst and seeing it everywhere, then getting predictably down in the dumps. What if you went to work expecting some stuff to go wrong, but also being highly confident in your capacity to let it go?

And by the way, it's easier to forgive in advance than trying to do it when tensions are high and rage is rising. If you wait till the moment of offense to decide what you're going to do with that boss, that client, or that colleague . . . then it's often too late to be who you want to be.

Decide in advance to forgive, and when the moment comes, you'll make the choices you really want.

5. CHOOSE TO MOVE FORWARD

Forgiveness is not forgetting; it's choosing to move forward. I've watched people bring bitterness into their current job that they picked up on their last job. It's been five years since the offense, and they're still making someone in the room pay for what someone who isn't in the room did.

It doesn't have to be that way. There can be life after hurt, after pain, after betrayal, after offense.

One friend of mine, a CPO (chief people officer), told me about a betrayal that happened to him years ago. He was working as a manager, and another company was considering him for a C-suite position. It was a dream job, and he was one of the final two candidates for the position. Toward the end of the interview process, the new company called the owner of his then-current company and asked him if he thought my friend was ready to be part of an executive team.

The owner said no.

The new company—based on that comment—chose the other candidate.

When my friend found out what happened, he couldn't believe it. He went to the owner and asked him why he said what he said. The answer was as simple as it was coldhearted.

"Because if they hired you, I'd have to find a new manager."

That's almost unforgivable, isn't it? The guy was willing to torpedo my friend's career out of sheer selfishness. Somehow, my friend had to move on. Eventually, he ended up getting hired at a great company, and that incident is now in the rearview mirror. But I can only imagine the pain and bitterness he had to deal with as he continued to work for a guy who had so callously stabbed him in the back.

I've heard other stories too. In my line of work, I meet with a lot of career business people, and some of the things that go on make me shake my head at humanity. One person told me how his partner ghosted him, took all the money, and fled to another country, never to be heard from again. I've met people who have lost millions due to someone else's actions, or who lost their life savings, or who were forced out of their jobs unfairly and never found a comparable job again. One person told me he was a C-suite executive, and his boss was manipulated into firing him. Now he's a junior-level manager making half as much, and every single paycheck is a reminder of how he got screwed over.

In my conversations with people, I've noticed that some people don't move on. They're walking around with an open wound, and it shows. Even minor offenses seem to trigger them. They spend a lot of energy on the unresolvable, immovable *whys* and *what ifs* that haunt them like ghosts. They've made a mental note to never trust again, never get close again, never let anyone in again. And their world has only gotten smaller as a result.

Often, they don't handle conflict well either. When they feel threatened, they either shoot first and ask questions later, or they roll over in surrender, assuming that yet again they've been taken advantage of. Neither of those knee-jerk, fight-or-flight reactions is healthy, but what else can you do when the past feels more real than the present, and the future might be worse than them all?

I've talked with others, like my CPO friend, who eventually did move on. These people might never be the same as they were before, and they might always feel a certain level of pain when they bring that offense to mind. But here's the thing—they don't bring it to mind very often. Somehow they've been able to shift their focus and their energy away from what somebody else did to them and toward what they can do now. They've kept their autonomy intact by taking ownership of what they can control: their reaction to what they've gone through.

I don't think anybody instantly moves on, by the way. Maybe some people seem to because they bury their feelings and forge ahead as if nothing happened, but that's not a great long-term strategy. Buried feelings, like zombies, tend to keep coming back.

The ability to rebound, adapt, and move forward from the harm we've been caused is one aspect of what's often termed *resilience,* which refers to your capacity to respond to stress and negative experiences in a healthy way. Resilience doesn't mean you never experience unpleasant emotions, but rather that you know what to do with those emotions when they show up. In general, when people who are less resilient go through a tough time, they tend to blame themselves more, overestimate how bad their life is, and view circumstances as permanent and unchangeable.[73]

I don't want those results. They sound terrible.

Forgiveness is one part of the solution. It enables you to work through the pain and come out whole on the other side. I'm interested in developing a greater "grudge resilience," if I can call it that. I want to get better at moving forward rather than being derailed by every complicated person or offensive action. Sure, it might take a hot minute to work through all my feelings, but I want to keep moving.

How resilient are you when hurt and offense come your way? Can you adapt? Can you bounce back? Can you process intense feelings in a healthy way? Can you move forward, even if you're still bleeding a little, still limping, still grieving what you've lost? Or will offense knock you off your feet and sweep you away in a tidal wave of negativity?

I know it's hard, and I know it feels unfair. But you can do hard things, and you can win at life even when it treats you unfairly.

CHOOSING TO MOVE FORWARD IS CHOOSING YOU.

It's making the decision that you need. The hurt and hate aren't helping. The bitterness and desire for revenge do nothing but leach your joy and peace. It's time to let that all go and step into the freedom found in forgiveness.

CHOOSE TO

BE the kind of colleague you want to be, regardless of how other people show up.

LET GO OF the small stuff, and remember that most of it is small stuff.

GIVE bitterness an expiration date rather than making it a lifelong companion.

FORGIVE people in advance, so that when complicated people do complicated things, you're ready.

AND MOST IMPORTANTLY,

CHOOSE TO keep moving forward, living fully and freely every day.

CONCLUSION

If I asked you to sum up this book in one word, what would it be?

COMPLICATED?

That would make sense. After all, I've used the word 435 times over twelve chapters. Plus, you probably work for a complicated company with complicated leaders making complicated decisions impacting complicated team members with complicated personalities and complicated personal lives living in a complicated world with complicated problems. So you've got "complicated" on your mind.

And yet, that's not the term I'm walking away with, and it's not the takeaway I hope you have either. If I had to pick one word to sum up all the research, experience, thought, and work that went into this book, it would be this:

HOPE.

There is hope for your cantankerous partner, for your problematic boss, for your aggravating employee. There is hope for your messy, sometimes painful interaction with that person. There is hope for you, because you are the one reading these words, which means you are serious about finding a way forward.

You might be in a place of frustration or desperation right now, but the story isn't over. I truly believe that if you engage with complicated individuals from a place of understanding, knowledge, and hope, you'll begin to see changes in your working relationship. You'll experience less friction and more freedom. You'll find ways to build bridges until you reach that wonderful, wide-open world of effective collaboration.

You can't put a timeline on it because humans are unpredictable and uncontrollable, but you can hope for it, and you can plan for it, and you can work toward it. Even if they don't change, you've changed, and you're continuing to do so. That alone can make a world of difference.

If you'd like to share your stories about working with complicated people, I'd love to hear them, and it will help guide our future research. Shoot me an email at info@ryanleak.com and as you tell your story, please "change the names to protect the innocent!" The good, the bad, the ugly, the funny, the tragic, the unbelievable . . . it's all part of being human, and it's all part of working with people.

The next time you walk your complicated self into your complicated workplace, do so with hope and confidence. You can make a difference, one interaction and one individual at a time.

ACKNOWLEDGMENTS

To my beautiful wife, Amanda, thank you for your unwavering support and love, especially when our schedule and life can be a little . . . complicated. Your presence is my anchor.

To my incredible kids, Jaxson and Roman, thank you for your boundless energy and endless inspiration. You remind me every day of the importance of curiosity, joy, and unconditional love.

To Jared Cagle, thank you for helping me build a plane in the air. Your flexibility and ingenuity have been crucial to making this project soar.

To McKenzie Decker, thank you for being the adult in the room who kept us on track with our actual goals for this book when we'd rather talk about sports. Your leadership has allowed us to accomplish way more than we could have ever imagined with this book.

To Chris Robinson, thank you for your positivity and influence along this journey. You've been incredibly generous with your insight and relationships, and your support has been crucial for this season of my life.

To Chad Johnson, thank you for being willing to put your name on the line for me. You didn't have to make all the connections that you have for me, but you rolled the dice on me several times, and I'll never forget it.

To Justin Jaquith, you are a gift from God in my life. This book would not exist without your brilliance. You helped take every idea I had to the next level. Thank you for meeting me at my pace to help this book become a reality.

To Whitney Gossett, thank you for being the kind of person who leverages all of their relationships to add value to other people. Your selflessness and connections have significantly impacted this book's journey.

To Jason Dorsey, thank you for coming alongside my team to research how to work with complicated people. Your insights for the book and for my career have been absolutely invaluable.

To Rory Vaden, thank you for teaching me the game of inches and helping me think outside of my comfort zone. Your wisdom has been transformative.

To Rodrigo Corral and your team, you changed my life. Thank you for helping me write more than just a book. You helped me see that we could give readers an experience. It's because of you that I want to be world-class in everything I do.

To Jen Gingerich and the Forefront Books squad, thank you so much for going with the flow on this project. Your editing, guidance, and insight along the way added so much value to this book.

To Shawn Hanks and the Premiere Speakers Bureau, thank you for trusting me with stages around the world to be able to help share this message.

To the Committee, I wouldn't be who I am without you. *Tashi deley.*

ENDNOTES

1. "The Employee Expectations Report 2022," Oyster, https://email.oysterhr.com/hubfs/The-Employee-Expectations-Report-2022.pdf.
2. Available at ryanleak.com. The research study was conducted online from February 6, 2024 to February 19, 2024. The margin of error is +/-3.1 percentage points.
3. Mel Robbins, Threads post, February 5, 2024, https://www.threads.net/@melrobbins/post/C2-7RgcRzxH.
4. Alain de Botton, "Why You Will Marry the Wrong Person," *New York Times*, May 28, 2016, https://www.nytimes.com/2016/05/29/opinion/sunday/why-you-will-marry-the-wrong-person.html.
5. Stephen M. R. Covey, *The Speed of Trust: The One Thing That Changes Everything* (Free Press, 2006), 13.
6. For example, see Arkadiusz M Jasiński and Romuald Derbis, "Work Stressors and Intention to Leave the Current Workplace and Profession: The Mediating Role of Negative Affect at Work," *International Journal of Environmental Research and Public Health* 19, no. 21 (October 27, 2022), 13992, https://doi.org/10.3390/ijerph192113992They conclude, "Interpersonal conflicts at work are the strongest predictor of negative affect at work."
7. Nicholas A. Christakis, and James H. Fowler, *Connected: The Surprising Power of Our Social Networks and How They Shape Our Lives* (Hachette UK, 2009), 28.
8. Donald Miller, *A Million Miles in a Thousand Years: What I Learned While Editing My Life* (Thomas Nelson, 2009), 206.
9. Chantel Prat, *The Neuroscience of You: How Every Brain Is Different and How to Understand Yours,* Kindle Edition (Penguin Publishing Group, 2022), 71.
10. Part, *The Neuroscience of You*, 3.
11. R. Nicholas Carleton, "Into the Unknown: A Review and Synthesis of Contemporary Models Involving Uncertainty," *Journal of Anxiety Disorders*, 39 (2016), 39, 10.1016/j.janxdis.2016.02.007.
12. Scott Gornto, *The Stories We Tell Ourselves* (Auxano Publishing, 2014), 15.
13. Brené Brown, *Rising Strong: How the Ability to Reset Transforms the Way We Live, Love, Parent, and Lead* (Random House, 2017), 122.
14. "Junior Achievement National Business Hall of Fame Recognizes Eight Outstanding Business Leaders," press release, February 25, 2000, Halstead Communications, https://www.newswise.com/articles/junior-achievement-national-business-hall-of-fame.

15. Mitchell Mannering, "The Sign of the Spear: The Story of William Wrigley, Who Made Spearmint Gum Famous," *National Magazine* (1912), https://todayinsci.com/W/Wrigley_William/WrigleyWilliam-NationalMagazineBio(1912).htm.
16. Quoted in "When Two Men in Business Always Agree, One of Them Is Unnecessary," quoteinvestigator.com, April 4, 2015, https://quoteinvestigator.com/2015/04/04/agree/.
17. Prat, *The Neuroscience of You,* 298.
18. "Mindset," merriam-webster.com/dictionary/mindset.
19. Gary Klein, "Mindsets: What They Are and Why They Matter," *Psychology Today*, blog post, May 1, 2016, https://www.psychologytoday.com/us/blog/seeing-what-others-dont/201605/mindsets.
20. In case you're curious how the other benefits we tested ranked, the results were: better communication (34%), better employee retention (30%), improved mental health (29%), increased engagement (27%), more focus (21%), greater trust in the company (18%), and increased innovation (12%).
21. M. R. Leary and N. R. Buttermore, "The Evolution of the Human Self: Tracing the Natural History of Self-Awareness," *Journal for the Theory of Social Behaviour* 33 (2003), 366.
22. See the discussion of Woolley et al, "Evidence for a Collective Intelligence Factor in the Performance of Human Groups," later in this chapter.
23. Steven Furtick, *Do the New You: 6 Mindsets to Become Who You Were Created to Be* (FaithWords, 2024), 25.
24. Michael Caire, Vamsy Reddy, and Matthew Varacallo, "Physiology, Synapse," updated March 27, 2023 (StatPearls Publishing, 2023), https://www.ncbi.nlm.nih.gov/books/NBK526047/#.
25. Human Brain Project, "Energy Efficiency of Neuromorphic Hardware Practically Proven," press release, May 24, 2022, https://www.humanbrainproject.eu/en/follow-hbp/news/2022/05/24/energy-efficiency-neuromorphic-hardware-practically-proven/.
26. Anita Williams Woolley, Christopher F. Chabris, Alex Pentland, Nada Hashmi, and Thomas W. Malone, "Evidence for a Collective Intelligence Factor in the Performance of Human Groups," *Science* 330 (October 29, 2010): 686–688.
27. Derek and Laura Cabrera, *Flock Not Clock: Design, Align, and Lead to Achieve Your Vision*, Kindle Edition (obb Plectica Publications, 2018), 21–22.
28. Howard Gardner, "There are 8 classes of intelligence. Which are you?," Big Think, https://bigthink.com/the-well/classes-of-intelligence/.
29. Patrick Heck et al. "65% of Americans Believe They Are Above average in Intelligence: Resuts of Two Nationally Representative Surveys," *PloS One* 13, no. 7 (July 3 2018): e0200103 https://www.ncbi.nlm.nih.gov/pmc/articles/PMC6029792/.
30. Cary Cherniss, Melissa Extein, Daniel Goleman, and Roger P. Weissberg, "Emotional Intelligence: What Does the Research Really Indicate?" *Educational Psychologist*, 41, no. 4 (2006): 240, https://doi.org/10.1207/s15326985ep4104_4.

31. Robert Cerone, "How (and Why) to Boost Your Adaptability Quotient," *Forbes.com*, December 20, 2019, https://www.forbes.com/sites/robertcerone/2019/12/20/how-and-why-to-boost-your-adaptability-quotient/?sh=4070758f6918.
32. Martin Reeves and Mike Deimler, "Adaptability: The New Competitive Advantage," *Harvard Business Review*, July–August 2011, 135–137.
33. Meryl Kornfield, Kim Bellware, and Hannah Knowles, "At First, Cat Lawyer Was Embarrassed. Then He Realized We All Could Use a Laugh," *The Washington Post*, February 9, 2021, https://www.washingtonpost.com/technology/2021/02/09/cat-lawyer-zoom-filter/.
34. Bill Boulding, "For Leaders, Decency Is Just as Important as Intelligence," *Harvard Business Review*, July 16, 2019, https://hbr.org/2019/07/for-leaders-decency-is-just-as-important-as-intelligence.
35. Stephen Trzeciak, Anthony Mazzarelli, and Emma Seppälä, "Leading with Compassion Has Research-Backed Benefits," *Harvard Business Review*, February 27, 2023, https://hbr.org/2023/02/leading-with-compassion-has-research-backed-benefits.
36. Cameron Anderson, Daron L. Sharps, Christopher J. Soto, and Oliver P. John, "People with Disagreeable Personalities (Selfish, Combative, and Manipulative) Do Not Have an Advantage in Pursuing Power at Work," *Proceedings of the National Academy of Sciences,* 117 no. 37 (August 202) 22780-22786, https://doi.org/10.1073/pnas.2005088117.
37. Peter, Laurence Jr., *Peter's Quotation Ideas for Our Times* (New York: William Morrow, 1977), 521.
38. Anita Lettink, "No, Millennials Will NOT Be 75% of the Workforce in 2025 (or Ever)!", blog post, September 16, 2019, https://www.linkedin.com/pulse/millennials-75-workforce-2025-ever-anita-lettink.
39. Emma Parry, Peter Urwin, "Generational Differences in Work Values: A Review of Theory and Evidence," *International Journal of Management Reviews* 13, no. 1 (2011): 79–96.
40. Michael Dimock, "Defining Generations: Where Millennials End and Generation Z Begins," Pew Research Center, January 17, 2019, https://www.pewresearch.org/short-reads/2019/01/17/where-millennials-end-and-generation-z-begins/.
41. Another respected research firm, the Center for Generational Kinetics, categorizes Gen X as 1965–1976, the Millennial generation as 1977–1995, and Gen Z as 1996–2015 (https://genhq.com/generational-birth-years/). For the sake of this chapter, I'll use the Pew Research Center's numbers, since the research that is available aligns more closely to those dates.
42. "An Intro to Generations," The Center for Generational Kinetics, 2023 https://genhq.com/the-generations-hub/generational-faqs/.
43. Frequently attributed, but the quote may be anonymous. See https://quoteinvestigator.com/2010/10/10/twain-father/ for further information.

44. Amy Cuddy, Michael Norton, and Susan Fiske, "This Old Stereotype: The Pervasiveness and Persistence of the Elderly Stereotype," *Journal of Social Issues,* 61, no. 2 (2005): 270.
45. Abraham Maslow, "A Theory of Human Motivation," *Psychological Review*, 50 (1943): 370–396.
46. Jennifer Robison, "Communicate Better with Employees, Regardless of Where They Work," Gallup, blog post, June 28, 2021, https://www.gallup.com/workplace/351644/communicate-better-employees-regardless-work.aspx
47. "The Biggest Problem in Communication Is the Illusion That It Has Taken Place," August 31, 2014, https://quoteinvestigator.com/2014/08/31/illusion/.
48. Ben McConnell, "Worst to First: How Mark Cuban Engineered a Team's Monumental Comeback," *MarketingProfs*, blog post, June 24, 2003, https://www.marketingprofs.com/3/huba6.asp.
49. "Clients or customers" clinched second place with 40%, followed by "managers or supervisors" (33%), "employees or direct reports" (22%), "executive or business owners" (16%), and "other" (3%).
50. K. Huang, M. Yeomans, A. W. Brooks, J. Minson, and F. Gino, "It Doesn't Hurt to Ask: Question-Asking Increases Liking," *Journal of Personality and Social Psychology,* 113, no. 3 (2017): 430–452, https://doi.org/10.1037/pspi0000097.
51. Inti Pacheco, "Nike to Lay Off More Than 1600 Workers," *The Wall Street Journal*, February 16, 2024, https://www.wsj.com/business/retail/nike-to-cut-over-1-600-jobs-14a97fd7.
52. Katherine Haan, "Remote Work Statistics and Trends in 2024," Forbes, June 12, 2023, https://www.forbes.com/advisor/business/remote-work-statistics/.
53. "Half of Companies Give Office Etiquette Classes as Workers Struggle with Appropriate Conversation, Dress," July 11, 2023, Resume Builder, https://www.resumebuilder.com/half-of-companies-give-office-etiquette-classes-as-workers-struggle-with-appropriate-conversation-dress/.
54. Samantha Masunaga, "We Don't Know How to Behave in the Office Anymore, Bosses Say. The solution? Charm School," *Los Angeles Times,* January 16, 2024, https://www.latimes.com/business/story/2024-01-16/back-to-the-office-bosses-are-sending-workers-to-etiquette-class
55. Karen Anding Fontenot, "Nonverbal Communic.ation and Social Cognition," *Salem Press Encyclopedia of Health, Research Starters* (Salem Press, 2023).
56. Kathy Dalpes, "5 Reasons Why the Customer Is Always Right," *Zendesk Blog*, March 4, 2024, https://www.zendesk.com.mx/blog/the-customer-is-always-right/#.
57. Lee Cockerell*, The Customer Rules: The 39 Essential Rules for Delivering Sensational Service* (The Crown Publishing Group, 2013), xiii.
58. Brené Brown, *Dare to Lead*, (Random House, 2019), 25.
59. Buc-ee's, "World Records" accessed July 15, 2025, https://buc-ees.com/about/world-record-holder/.

60. Steve Tobak, "Leadership Lessons from BlackBerry's Demise," MoneyWatch, CBS News, April 12, 2012, https://www.cbsnews.com/news/leadership-lessons-from-blackberrys-demise/.
61. Raoul Davis, "How Ego Tanks Branding and Marketing Professionals' Progress And Jeopardizes Companies," *Forbes.com,* blog post, Oct. 23, 2017, https://www.forbes.com/sites/forbesagencycouncil/2017/10/23/how-ego-tanks-branding-and-marketing-professionals-progress-and-jeopardizes-companies/?sh=7df1f1764088.
62. "Workplace Conflict and How Businesses Can Harness It to Thrive," CPP Global Human Capital Report, July 2008, https://www.themyersbriggs.com/-/media/f39a8b7fb4fe4daface552d9f485c825.ashx.
63. Emmanuel Acho, Instagram post, September 27, 2023, https://www.instagram.com/emmanuelacho/reel/CxtbL15SCMZ/.
64. Katie Shonk, "3 Types of Conflict and How to Address Them: Program on Negotiation," Harvard Law School, blog post, December 14, 2023, https://www.pon.harvard.edu/daily/conflict-resolution/types-conflict/.
65. Karen A. Jehn and Elizabeth A. Mannix, "The Dynamic Nature of Conflict: A Longitudinal Study of Intragroup Conflict and Group Performance," *Academy of Management Journal* 44, no. 2 (2001): 238, https://doi.org/10.5465/3069453. Jehn and Mannix include values as part of relational conflict and separate task conflict into two categories: task and process.
66. Henry Cloud, *Necessary Endings: The Employees, Businesses, and Relationships That All of Us Have to Give Up in Order to Move Forward* (HarperCollins, 2011), 8.
67. David Goggins, *Can't Hurt Me: Master Your Mind and Defy the Odds* (Lioncrest Publishing, 2018), 342.
68. Joe Sanok, "A Guide to Setting Better Boundaries," *Harvard Business Review*, blog post, April 14, 2022, https://hbr.org/2022/04/a-guide-to-setting-better-boundaries.
69. Rebecca Ray, "Episode 34, Boundary Creep, Boundary Errors, and Boundary Violations in Business," podcast show notes, https://rebeccaray.com.au/episode-34/.
70. James Clear, "3-2-1: On Muddy Puddles and Leaky Ceilings, the Secret to Productivity, and How to Spoil a Great Relationship," blog post, March 28, 2024, https://jamesclear.com/3-2-1/march-28-2024.
71. Wenrui Cao, Reine C. van der Wal, Toon W. Taris, "The Benefits of Forgiveness at Work: A Longitudinal Investigation of the Time-Lagged Relations Between Forgiveness and Work Outcomes," *Front. Psychol.* 12 (2021): https://doi.org/10.3389/fpsyg.2021.710984.
72. Eric Jaffe, "The Complicated Psychology of Revenge," Association for Psychological Science, October 4, 2011, https://www.psychologicalscience.org/observer/the-complicated-psychology-of-revenge.
73. Bill Kte'pi, "Resilience (Psychology)," *Salem Press Encyclopedia, Research Starters* (Salem Press, 2023).